From Workshop to Empire

Britain 1750–1900

Hamish Macdonald

Stanley Thornes (Publishers) Ltd

Text © Hamish Macdonald 1995

Designed and typeset by Hilary Norman
Illustrations by Beverley Curl, Hardlines and Tim Smith
Cover artwork by Lee Montgomery, Beehive Illustration
Picture research by Julia Hanson

Original illustrations © Stanley Thornes (Publishers) Ltd 1995

First published in 1995 by:
Stanley Thornes (Publishers) Ltd
Ellenborough House
Wellington Street
CHELTENHAM GL50 1YW
England
99 00 0102 / 10 9 8 7 6 5 4 3 2
A catalogue record for this book is available from the British
Library.

ISBN 0–7487–1931–8

Printed in Hong Kong

Acknowledgements

The author and publishers are grateful to the
following for permission to reproduce illustrations
and photographs in this book.

Aerofilms Ltd, 6; Bridgeman Art Library, 5, 41
(Top) (British Library), 38 (Cheltenham Art Gallery
and Museums), 40, 72, 73 (City of Bristol Museum
and Art Gallery), 40 (Bottom) (Guildhall Library,
Corporation of London), 60 (Bottom) (Manchester
City Art Gallery), 69 (Museum of London), 50
(Bottom) (Royal Holloway and Bedford New
College), 83 (TUC, London); Bristol Record Office,
74, 75 (Top); British Library, 70, 85, 27 (India
Office Collection); British Museum, 79; John Carter
Brown Library, Brown University, 28; Derby City
Art Gallery and Museums/Private Collection, 53,
54; Edifice, 43; Freer Gallery of Art, Washington
DC, USA, 25; Hulton Deutsch Collection, 16, 50
(Top), 55, 64, 95 (Bottom L); Ironbridge Gorge
Museum Trust: Elton Collection, 52; Mansell
Collection, 8, 26, 31, 36, 41, 45, 59, 61, 62, 63,
68, 71, 80, 81, 82, 84, 86, 99, 106–7; Mary Evans
Picture Library, 47, 65, 66, 75, 104–5, 46 (Bruce
Castle Museum); National Army Museum, 33, 35;
National Library of Australia, 67; National Library
of Ireland, 9 (Top); National Maritime Museum, 19;
National Motor Museum, 52; National Museum of
Labour History, 108, 111; Peter Newark Historical
Pictures, 38; Royal Archives, © HM the Queen
1995, 18; Royal Geographical Society, 51; Royal
Naval Museum, 34; Sheffield City Art Gallery, 58;
Thompson, Dorothy (from *Queen Victoria: Gender and
Power*, Virago, 1990) 15; Trustees of the British
Museum, 9 (Bottom R) , 12, 13, 14, 17, 29; Yale
University (Print Collection, Lewis Walpole Library),
9 (Bottom L).

Every effort has been made to contact copyright
holders and we apologise if any have been
overlooked.

Contents

1 Transformations

How much did Britain change between 1750 and 1900?

In the years between 1750 and 1900 events and people made many changes to Britain. They changed the way parts of the countryside looked, the way people travelled, how they dressed, what they ate and even the inside of their homes.

Britain became the United Kingdom of England, Wales, Scotland and Ireland. The number of people living in the United Kingdom grew from about 9.5 million to 41 million. Complete changes or transformations were caused by new methods of farming and the demand for more workers to mine for coal, make iron, work in factories and build new roads, canals and railways. The sudden speed of these transformations in farming and industry came to be called the Agricultural and Industrial Revolutions.

They happened in Britain before any other country and transformed Britain into the richest and most powerful country in the world. By 1900 most people in Britain lived in towns instead of the countryside. People demanded and won more say in who governed them. As a result there were changes in the way the poor were looked after, laws were passed to improve supplies of clean water and disposal of rubbish and sewage, and a police force for the whole country was created. Transformations like these also caused problems. While some people became very rich many people were poor. Poor living conditions led to a big increase in outbreaks of disease and crime.

Source A 1750

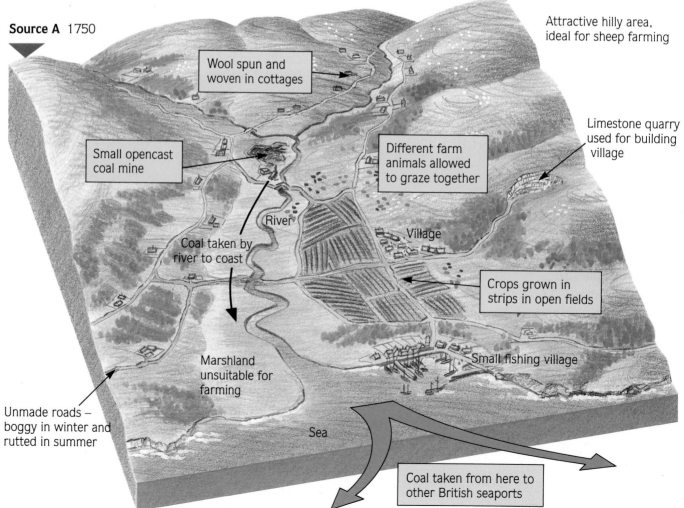

Attractive hilly area, ideal for sheep farming

Wool spun and woven in cottages

Limestone quarry used for building village

Small opencast coal mine

Different farm animals allowed to graze together

River

Village

Coal taken by river to coast

Crops grown in strips in open fields

Marshland unsuitable for farming

Small fishing village

Unmade roads – boggy in winter and rutted in summer

Sea

Coal taken from here to other British seaports

Source B 1900

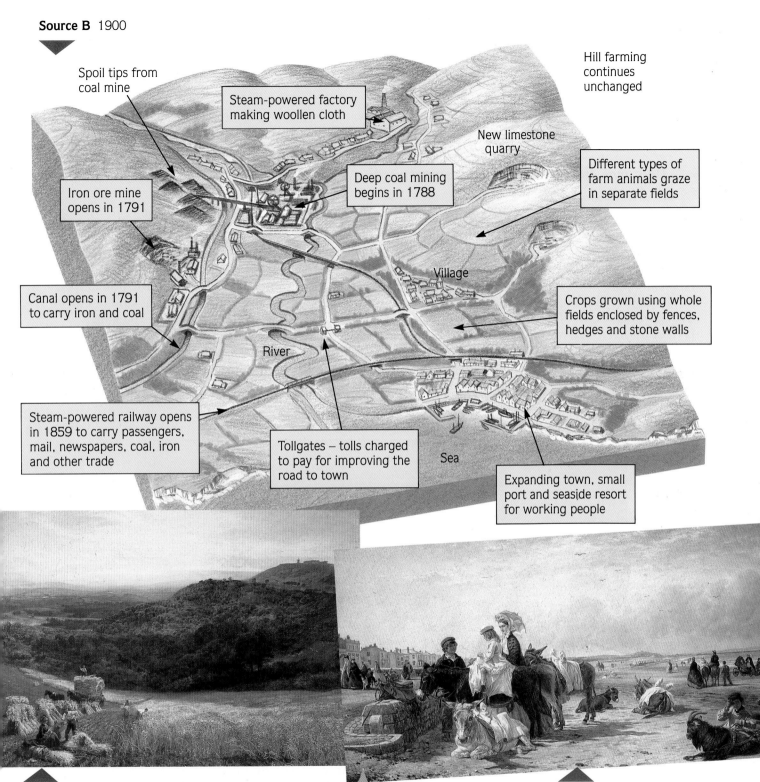

Spoil tips from coal mine

Steam-powered factory making woollen cloth

Hill farming continues unchanged

New limestone quarry

Different types of farm animals graze in separate fields

Iron ore mine opens in 1791

Deep coal mining begins in 1788

Canal opens in 1791 to carry iron and coal

Village

Crops grown using whole fields enclosed by fences, hedges and stone walls

Steam-powered railway opens in 1859 to carry passengers, mail, newspapers, coal, iron and other trade

River

Tollgates – tolls charged to pay for improving the road to town

Sea

Expanding town, small port and seaside resort for working people

Source C Harvest Time

Source D Weston Sands

Investigations

1 Spot the differences between Sources **A** and **B** for 1750 and 1900. Try to find two differences for each of the following: farming, industry, transport.

2 Make a list of changes between 1750 and 1900 not shown in Sources **A** and **B**. Use the written information on Transformations to help you.

3 Find a partner. Take it in turns for one of you to describe and the other to write down who you can see and what is happening in Sources **C** and **D**.

4 Sources **C** and **D** were painted in the 1860s. Use the information in Sources **A** and **B** to:
a) find one clue in **C** which shows this was painted between 1750 and 1900.
b) explain why it became easier for working people in **D** to spend their holidays by the seaside at this time.

5

2 A United Kingdom?
Government

Who governed?

In 1750 a German who did not speak English well, called King George II, ruled the United Kingdom of England, Wales and Scotland. To help him govern he chose a small group of men, called ministers. The most important of these ministers was the First Lord of the Treasury who came to be called the prime minister. George II gave the prime minister a house at 10 Downing Street in London which became his official home. Here the prime minister met the other ministers in a private room called a cabinet where they helped make all the important decisions.

The ministers, and more often the prime minister, would meet and advise the king at one of his own homes in or near London. The king's official London home was St James's Palace but later King George III (1760-1820) preferred to use Buckingham house, where Buckingham Palace now stands, as his main London home.

Source A
An aerial view of Westminster, London

Buckingham Palace

St James's Palace

Downing Street

The Houses of Parliament

How much did the government do?

The government at the end of the eighteenth century did a lot less than the government does today. It did look after how the taxpayers' money was spent, law and order, defence and foreign trade. It took no interest in looking after the poor, the unemployed, the sick or the old, or in education.

How important was Parliament in 1750?

Two important laws set limits to the power of the monarch and his government: the Bill of Rights (1689) and the Act of Settlement (1701). The Bill of Rights said the monarch had to obey laws which could be made only with the help of Parliament. He could not raise money by taxes or have an army without the permission of Parliament. The Act of Settlement allowed only a Protestant who belonged to the Church of England to become monarch. The monarch could not sack judges, leave England, or take England to war to defend another country without Parliament's permission.

'Parliament' comes from the Latin word meaning to talk. In 1750 only about one in 12 adult males had the right to vote for a member of parliament (MP) to speak for them in the House of Commons. Most nobles in the House of Lords inherited the right to be there. However, the monarch had the power to create new nobles and appointed bishops of the Church of England. The two Houses of Parliament met together in the Palace of Westminster. If MPs strongly disliked the monarch's choice of a minister they could force the king to sack him but this rarely happened.

Political parties

No proper political parties existed at this time. Politicians sided together in small groups called factions if they felt the need to put pressure on the government or to defend it from its enemies. There were also powerful political families such as the Pelhams, Grenvilles, Bedfords and Rockinghams. They competed for the favour of the king to become ministers in his government or opposed the government if they disliked its policies.

People liked to label politicians either 'Whigs' or 'Tories'. However, during most of King George III's reign (1760-1820) there was little real difference between them. When politicians began to organise strong political parties in the second part of the nineteenth century, Whigs became the Liberal party and Tories became the Conservative party.

Investigations

1 Use Source **A** to name the places marked at A, B, C and D on this street plan.

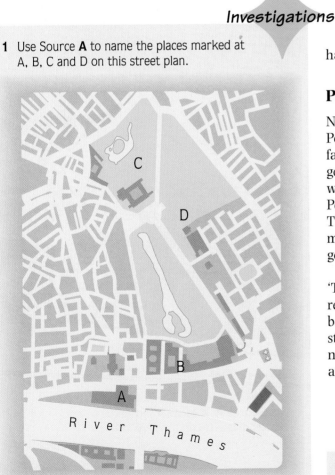

R i v e r   T h a m e s

a) How important was A in 1750?
b) Why do you think C was built?
c) Whose official home is in B?

2 Who do you think had the most power in eighteenth century government: the monarch or the House of Commons? Explain your answer.

Remember...

- England was governed by a monarch with the help of ministers he chose himself.

- The government did not do as much as governments do today and depended on the support of Parliament.

- There were no proper political parties at this time.

7

Power

Whoever owned land had power and influence. By 1750 rich families already owned large estates. However, a number of extremely wealthy businessmen, merchants, bankers and lawyers bought land during the eighteenth century. The wealthy brewer, Samuel Whitbread, used the profits of his business to buy 12 000 acres of good farmland in Bedfordshire in 1762.

Landowners controlled most of the seats or places in the House of Commons. They did this in two ways. Some, like Samuel Whitbread, bought their way into the House of Commons. Others used their wealth to help people they liked become MPs - a form of favouritism called **patronage**. Sir James Lowther, who gained his wealth from land and coal mines, was the **patron** of 8 MPs in Cumberland and Westmorland.

Landowners told voters who rented land from them or who worked for them who to vote for. To qualify to vote it was necessary in most cases to either own or rent property. Voters had to show how they voted in front of people instead of being allowed to keep this a secret. It was common to bribe and threaten voters. A very large number of MPs did not have to face an election contest. MPs were not paid and so had to be either wealthy or to have rich patrons like Sir James Lowther.

Source A A cartoon showing a candidate trying to win votes

Show of Hands for a Liberal Candidate.

Remember...

- In 1750 power and influence came from owning land.

- Usually only property holders could vote.

- Many voters had little real choice about who to vote for.

- To become an MP it was necessary to be either wealthy or have a rich patron.

Investigations

1 **a)** Look on and under the platform in Source **A**. Describe three things used to win votes in this election.
 b) Give three ways in which voting in an election is different today.

2 How did someone become an MP in 1750?

Key words

Patronage The power to give jobs and privileges.

8

Divisions within the United Kingdom

The Union

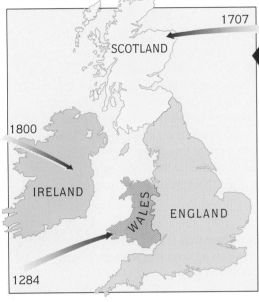

Source A The stages in the making of the United Kingdom

England conquered Wales in 1284 and passed an Act of Union in 1536. Another Act of Union in 1707 linked Scotland with England making one United Kingdom called Great Britain. Ireland was added in 1800. It was a less than happy union. Many people resented being ruled by a parliament far away in London but any resistance to it was brutally crushed. To this day many Welsh, Scots and Irish dislike the Union.

Source B An English cartoon of a Scotsman which appeared in *North Briton*, a political newspaper, in 1763

Source C An Irish cartoon commenting on the behaviour of British soldiers in 1798

Religious conflict

The Union was for political and religious reasons. Religion, however, continued to divide the country. The monarch had to promise to defend the 'established' or official faith of the Church of England against both Protestant and Roman Catholic enemies. Protestants who did not belong to the Church of England (called **Dissenters** and **Nonconformists**) had cause to resent laws - Corporation Acts (1661) and the Test Act (1673) - which banned them and Roman Catholics from having government jobs or becoming MPs. In 1780 a godson of King George II, Lord George Gordon, stirred up a violent attack on Roman Catholics and their property (Source **D**). This resulted in the biggest fire in London since 1666 and over 300 deaths.

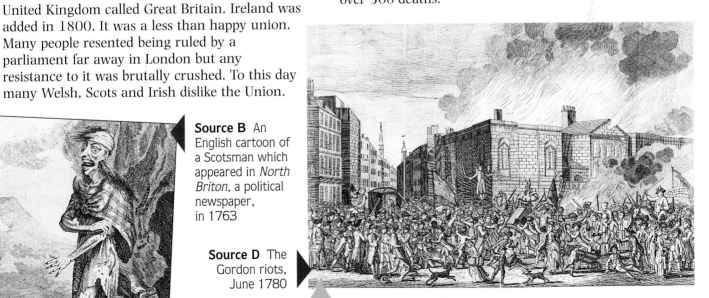

Source D The Gordon riots, June 1780

Key words

Dissenter A Protestant who refuses to accept the monarch as the head of the Church or to belong to the Church of England.
Nonconformist Another name for a dissenter.

Poverty and rough justice

London was the United Kingdom's only very large city. The second largest was Bristol which was a tenth of the size of London. Many of the 750 000 people who lived in London were desperately poor (Source **E**).

Source E Gin Lane, St Giles, London

Poverty and hardship all over the United Kingdom led to sympathy with the revolutionaries in France who in 1793 executed their king, Louis XVI. On 29 October 1795 an angry crowd hissed and hooted King George III on his way to open Parliament. They pelted his carriage, cracking a window.

Most people lived in the countryside. High bread prices and changes which took people's jobs led to riots, the smashing of machinery and burning of property. It was the job of the Lord-Lieutenants of the Counties to send in soldiers to keep law and order. They chose landowners to be Justices of the Peace (JPs) who decided how to punish people. Debt was a crime punished by a prison sentence. Rioting,

poaching, picking pockets, stealing a loaf of bread or a handkerchief were hanging offences even for children. However, in practice, alternatives to hanging for such crimes became more usual, such as transportation for life to a prison colony in Australia.

Communication

There were five different languages spoken in the United Kingdom: Scots Gaelic, Irish Gaelic, Welsh, Cornish and English. Though English was the most widely used language, different versions, called dialects, and strong regional accents divided the country into separate communities with their own traditions. Without railways, telephones or the radio (none of which had been invented) news travelled slowly and it was not possible to have a national newspaper or even keep to a national time - local time varied from village to village. It was not unusual to find people who had not travelled more than 15 miles from their homes in their whole lives.

Remember

- The English government created the United Kingdom against the wishes of many Scots, Irish and Welsh.

- Religious minorities did not have the same rights as those who belonged to the Protestant Church of England.

- There were extremes of wealth and poverty and a harsh system of justice.

- Language and cultural differences separated communities.

- Methods of transport and communication were slow.

Investigations

1   a)   In what ways are Sources **B** and **C** (page 9) biased?
    b)   What do these cartoons suggest about England's relations with the Scots and Irish?

2   a)   Why were the 'Gordon' riots so called?
    b)   Source **D** shows Newgate prison on fire. For what other reason does this suggest people joined in the riots?

3   a)   Look at Source **E**. Describe the problems which the artist thought were caused by gin drinking.
    b)   What other causes were there of problems like these?

4   'The United Kingdom was not united.' Find one reason a) to agree and b) to disagree with this point of view.

Depth Study: The image and role of the royal family

Source A Family tree of the Hanover royal family. George III became king in 1760. He reigned for 60 years

George I m. Sophia Dorothea (1714–27)

Monarchs who ruled in their own right

m. married to

George II m. Caroline of Brandenburg-Anspach (1727–60)

Frederick Louis m. Augusta of Saxe-Gotha Prince of Wales (died 1751)

William Duke of Cumberland

and others

George III m. Charlotte of Mecklenburg-Strelitz (1760–1820)

George IV m. Caroline of (1820–30) Brunswick

Frederick Duke of York (died 1827)

William IV m. Adelaide of (1830–37) Saxe-Meiningen

Edward Duke m. Victoria of of Kent Saxe-Coburg

Ernest Augustus King of Hanover

and others

Victoria m. Albert of Saxe-Coburg (1837–1901)

Victoria m. Frederick III Princess of Germany Royal

Edward VII m. Alexandra (1901–10) of Denmark

Alice

Alfred Duke of Edinburgh

Helena

Louise

Arthur Duke of Connaught

Leopold Duke of Albany

Beatrice m. Henry of Battenberg

Albert Duke of Clarence (died 1892)

George V (1910–36)

Louise

Victoria

Maud m. Haakon VII of Norway

11

What good things did people say about King George III?

- He was the first British king to study science as a boy.
- He took a keen interest in new methods of farming which earned him the nickname 'Farmer George'.
- He could play the violin, flute and harpsichord.
- He was a faithful husband.

What did critics say about King George III?

- They said his mother dominated him. She made sure he married a dull German princess instead of the woman he loved.
- They accused him of favouritism and of using his power of patronage to get his own way with Parliament.
- They blamed him for losing the American War of Independence and the American colonies (see pages 22 and 28).
- From 1788 they said he was mad.

One fierce critic was the **radical** MP, John Wilkes.

Source B
John Wilkes, MP for Middlesex, with copies of *North Briton* and holding up a cap of liberty

Source C John Wilkes used his newspaper, the *North Briton*, to stir up public opinion with daring comments like:

> The King is only the first **magistrate**...of this country...responsible to his people for the due exercise of the Royal function in the choice of his ministers.
>
> **From No 45 of the *North Briton*, April 1763**

George's ministers had Wilkes arrested, expelled from Parliament and put in prison. By treating Wilkes like a criminal for writing and saying what he thought George just increased Wilkes' popularity. A court of law ruled that George's government was in the wrong. The voters of Middlesex repeatedly elected Wilkes as their MP. In the end angry protests forced King George to back down.

Look at Source **C** again. Wilkes aimed his criticism not just at King George but at his ministers. George's first choice of prime minister was the Scottish Earl of Bute who was a close friend of his mother. Bute was so unpopular he was soon forced to resign. There were several more changes of government until in 1770 Lord North became prime minister. He lasted until 1782. It was during this time that Britain lost the American colonies after a revolution and the war of American Independence.

King George then had to struggle again to form a strong government. In 1783 he chose the Duke of Portland as prime minister. He had to allow an old enemy, Charles James Fox, to become foreign secretary, a sign that the monarch had lost more power. Fox tried to get Parliament's support for a plan for 'a better government' of the lands ruled by the East India trading company. George did not like this. So, taking the advice of an ambitious young politician, William Pitt, he let the House of Lords know that he would consider anyone who voted for Fox's plan as a personal enemy. The Lords obeyed and threw out the plan. Within a month William Pitt was prime minister.

The most dangerous years of his reign began with the French Revolution in 1789.

Key words

Enlightened country Country whose people believe that humans are born equal and have rights to a fair system of government.

Magistrate Someone with power to enforce the law.
Radical Someone who favours thorough political and social changes.

Source D Tom Paine was an Englishman who supported and helped both the American and French revolutionaries. In 1792 he wrote,

> I do not believe that monarchy and aristocracy will continue seven years longer in any of the **enlightened countries** of Europe.
>
> From *The Rights of Man, Part 2*, 1792

Source E A cartoon showing George III as 'A connoisseur [expert] examining a Cooper'

A CONNOISSEUR examining a COOPER.

Source **E** shows King George III in 1792 examining a small portrait of Oliver Cromwell by the famous artist Samuel Cooper. Britain had tried being a republic before France, between 1649 to 1653, but this had ended badly with a military dictatorship set up by Oliver Cromwell which lasted until 1660. By 1792 King George III had been king of Britain for 30 years. Within a year of this date the revolutionaries in France had executed their king and had declared war on Britain. George survived as king until he died 30 years later.

Did King George really go mad?

George was seriously ill in 1788, 1801, 1804 and from 1810.

Today it is known that King George suffered from a rare disease called porphyria. The symptom which gives the most important clue is the colour of the urine. This is caused by the body producing too much of the pigment which gives blood its colour. It poisons the nervous system and the brain.

Source F

Symptoms	Diagnosis	Treatments
Fever High pulse rate Stomach cramps	'Evil Humours'	14 ounces of blood drawn off from a vein in the foot
Fits		A straitjacket.
A rash on the back Purple or red urine Unable to listen to music Violent behaviour Bursting into tears		Feet and legs blistered with Spanish Fly (made from the dried bodies of beetles) to draw out the ill-humour. Trip to Cheltenham to drink spa waters.
Talking to trees Babbling Loss of sight		Trip to Weymouth to drink and swim in sea water.

Investigations

1 Look at Source **A** on page 11. Name three kings and one queen of England between 1750 and 1900.

2 Use the information to find and explain one or two clues in Source **B** which suggest that John Wilkes was popular for criticising King George III?

3 What does Source **E** suggest King George III was afraid of?

4 Look at Source **F**.
a) Which symptom of George III's illness is shown in Source **E**?
b) How might doctors today have treated King George differently from the doctors in the eighteenth century?

What image did people have of George III's sons?

King George III's health became so bad by 1811 that his son, George, took over as ruler (**Regent**) until his father's death in 1820. George III's sons were not popular. They were rude, lazy and ran up huge debts.

The image people had of the behaviour of the Prince Regent and his brothers is shown in Source **G**. It shows the princes with their mistresses. George, Prince of Wales, is in the centre dancing with his daughter, Charlotte, and his illegal wife, Mrs Fitzherbert. Mrs Fitzherbert was a Roman Catholic widow who refused to become George's mistress. George ignored laws which said that the heir to the throne could not marry a Roman Catholic and that he had to have the King's permission to marry. He married Mrs Fitzherbert secretly in 1785 and she had several of his children. In the cartoon his legal wife, Caroline, whom he was forced to marry in 1775, is leaving the room deserted and unhappy. In the far left corner one of George's mistresses, Lady Hertford, is playing with political puppets who represent the real politicians she controlled. Playing cards with their mistresses are two of George's brothers, William, the Duke of Clarence and Frederick, the Duke of York. William's mistress was the actress Mrs Jordan who had 11 of his illegitimate children. To the right another brother, the Duke of Sussex lusts after Mrs Billington. She is playing the piano while he stands on the portrait of his deserted secret wife, Lady Augusta Murray.

Source G   A cartoon of the royal family, 1812

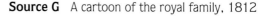

PRINCELY AMUSEMENTS OR THE HUMORS OF THE FAMILY.

Key words

Bigamist A man who has an illegal second wife.
Regent Person who carries out the duties of a ruler when the monarch is too young, too ill or unable to rule.

Investigations

1 Use the family tree (Source **A**) to work out which future kings of England are shown in Source **G**?

2 How is each behaving and when did each become king?

Queen Victoria

Victoria was the daughter of Prince Edward, the Duke of Kent. Of all George III's 15 children she was the only legitimate grandchild to survive. She became queen in 1837 at the age of 19. By this time the image of the royal family was at its lowest point. George IV, William IV, and her father the Duke of Kent were **bigamists** and unfaithful husbands who wasted the taxpayers' money and sponged off their friends. During her long reign Queen Victoria and her family were not always popular either. Her marriage to her cousin, Albert of Saxe-Coburg in 1840 provoked two kinds of prejudice which are shown in Source **H**.

Her husband was unpopular because he was a foreigner. She was thought not capable of ruling because she was a woman. By hard work and by being an excellent husband Albert eventually won respect. Together they helped create a model image of the family shown in Source **I**. They had nine children.

Source H Cartoon of Victoria and Albert from a popular magazine

KING ALBERT SAXE-HUMBUG.   QUEEN VIC.

A German to be Regent raises John Bull's gall,
But to try on Britain's *Crown* CROWNS all!

For young Misses to rule 'twas surely never meant,
But 'tis plain we are now under a Miss-government.

Source I An illustration from *A Book of English Song* (1842) showing the royal family

ILLUSTRATED BOOK OF BRITISH SONG.

GOD SAVE THE QUEEN.

Albert died of typhoid in 1861. Queen Victoria was so upset that she withdrew from public life which made her unpopular. Once again there was talk of England getting rid of the monarchy and becoming a republic. Even senior politicians like Joseph Chamberlain held these views. Most official photographs show her unsmiling and she always wore black as a sign of mourning for her husband. Nevertheless, there were strong rumours that she found another companion, a Scottish servant (or 'gillie') called John Brown (Source **J**). This explains how she got the popular nickname, 'Mrs Brown'.

Source J A cartoon of John Brown from a cheap magazine

15

How close their relationship was will never be known exactly because her family destroyed many of her diaries when she died.

Victoria always took a close interest in politics. Her favourite prime ministers were Lord Melbourne, Robert Peel, and Benjamin Disraeli. She disliked Lord Palmerston and William Gladstone. Disraeli encouraged her back into public life by what he described as flattery 'with a trowel'. In 1876 he created the title, 'Empress of India' for her.

Source **K** is a rare photograph which shows her smiling. She had a sense of humour and enjoyed drinking Scotch whisky which she sometimes mixed with claret.

Source K
Victoria in 1898

Source L A description of Victoria by an MP

> S he laughs in real earnest, opening her mouth as wide as it can go, showing not very pretty gums...she eats quite as heartily as she laughs, I think I may say she gobbles.
>
> **From the diary of Thomas Creevey, MP, 1802-1838**

When she died in 1901 her body was laid in her coffin on top of a plaster cast of Albert's hand, his dressing gown and family photographs.

Her son, Albert Edward, Prince of Wales, had to wait until he was 61 to become king. His life style worried her a good deal. Source **M** is a comment on the embarrassment he caused her.

Source N Description by the Queen's doctor of how he arranged her body

> p ut in the Queen's left hand the photo of Brown and his hair in a case (according to her private instructions), which I wrapped in tissue paper and covered with Queen Alexandra's flowers.
>
> **From the diary of Sir James Reid**

Source M Cartoon of Victoria and her son, 'L'enfant terrible', printed in the *Evening Standard* newspaper

Investigations

1 With a partner study Sources **H** to **N**. Decide which sources people living at the time
   a) would have known about
   b) would not have known about.

2 Divide a page into two columns with headings like this:

Images of Queen Victoria

A Good image	B Not a good image

In column A give dates when Victoria's image was good and describe her image. In column B give dates when Victoria's image and her family's image were not good and explain why.

Why did the monarchy survive?

King George III wanted to be a good king. He saw the system of government as a kind of political clock which he described as:

> The most beautiful combination ever framed.

This agreed with the expert on government, Sir William Blackstone, who explained it as a system of checks and balances:

Source P

> All the parts of it form a mutual check upon each other. In the legislature [Parliament] the people [Commons] are a check upon the nobility [Lords]...while the king is a check upon both.
>
> **Commentaries on the Laws of England, 1787**

The monarchy survived during George III's reign because he meant well despite being aggressive and clumsy sometimes when dealing with people. His attempts to have his own way over Parliament made the opposition more organised and proved that, in reality, his powers were limited. Towards the end of his reign his illness made him seem even more harmless. From 1793 to 1794 news of mass executions by the revolutionaries in France reached England. This led to a patriotic revival of support for the monarchy.

Investigations

Look at Source **Q**.
a) What is happening to the Speaker?
b) Who do you think the people in chains are?
c) What does the artist think would be the consequences of a French invasion?

Source Q Cartoon by Gillray in 1798 showing what many English people feared would happen if the French revolutionaries took over England. The man in the centre in front of the big chair is called the Speaker. The Speaker keeps order in, and speaks for, the House of Commons

What is more surprising is that the monarchy survived the reigns of George III's sons, George IV and William IV. Queen Victoria and her husband did much to restore respect for the monarchy. By 1901 the power of the monarch to interfere in government was much less than it had been in 1801. This was a result of giving more people the right to vote and the growth of strong political parties which made Parliament stronger. However, the role of the monarch in foreign affairs remained very powerful. As Source **R** shows Queen Victoria was related to the most powerful royal families in Europe.

Source R Queen Victoria with English, German and Russian royalty at a family wedding in Coburg in April 1894. Seated on the left is Kaiser Wilhelm II of Germany. Standing to his right is Tsar Nicholas II of Russia

Investigations

1 This is a drawing of a seesaw with a person (C) standing on it:

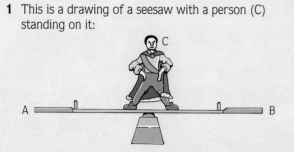

A, B, and C help to check and balance each other. Read Source **P**. Then draw the seesaw. Label A, 'The Commons'; label B, 'The Lords'.

Who do you think C is supposed to be? Give a reason for your answer.

2 **a)** Why was there a possibility that the monarchy would not survive between 1760 and 1901?
b) Why do you think the monarchy did survive?

3 **a)** Name two important relatives of Queen Victoria shown in Source **R**.
b) What power and influence does Source **R** suggest that the monarchy still had in 1901?

3 A sea-trading empire?

Protection of trade

Was there a need to protect trade?

By 1760 Britain was the leading trading nation. Also it seemed that Britain was fast becoming the top manufacturing nation - 'the workshop of the world'. Though Britain's resources and island position gave her natural advantages over other countries (see Source **D** on page 20) it was thought necessary to protect British traders from foreign competition.

Trade was protected in the following ways:
- Traders joined together and formed **joint-stock companies** to share the costs and risks.
- Some companies, like the East India Company, obtained royal charters to give them 'legal' rights to trade without competition.
- Special laws, called Navigation Laws (1651, 1660), gave British merchants advantages over foreign competitors: all trade with Britain had to be carried in British merchant ships; all colonies had to involve Britain before trading with other countries.
- Britain banned or charged heavy customs **duties** on **imports** from rivals like France.

What was the case for protection?

Britain's success as a trading nation depended on buying raw materials from overseas to make things with and then selling the finished products to markets overseas. Protection helped British traders survive against competition from foreign markets. Traders took big risks:
- ships and cargoes could be lost at sea.
- wars could upset trade.
- profits could be lost if foreign traders or smugglers brought cheaper goods into Britain.

Was there a case against protection?

A Scottish university professor, Adam Smith (Sources **A** and **B**), argued in 1776 that protection of trade was a bad thing. He believed that competition encouraged more trade. He criticised traders like the East India Company for using protection to keep prices high.

Source A Adam Smith said that traders were…

> men whose interest is never exactly the same with that of the public.

Source B Adam Smith believed that by protecting trade the government acted…

> for the defence of the rich against the poor.
> **From The Wealth of Nations, 1776**

Source C A fleet of British merchant ships of the East India Company

Key words

Duties Taxes, especially on goods from foreign countries.
Imports Goods bought from a different country.

Joint-stock company A company formed by putting the money (stock) of traders together.

Source D Britain's natural advantages

Forests

Wood for building and fuel

Entrepreneurs

Wealthy businessmen looking for ideas and inventions to back to make money

Mild climate

Good for farming and textile industries (linen, wool, cotton)

Rivers
- Inland transport
- Water power

Centres of learning
◆ Ideas for improving trade e.g. Adam Smith's Wealth of Nations

Excellent farm land
- Good food supply
- Wool

Good supply of minerals

c Coal
i Iron

Surrounded by sea
- A natural defence against enemies
- Good for overseas trade in all directions

Edinburgh
Cambridge
Oxford
LONDON

Strong government

Kept Britain united, stable and peaceful

Growing population

A large, cheap labour force

Remember...

- **Britain had natural advantages over other countries.**
- **British traders were protected from competition.**
- **Some people began to think that protection of trade was bad for Britain.**

Investigations

1 Which three natural advantages do you think were the most important for trade? Explain your choice.

2 Which ways of protecting trade would Adam Smith have disapproved of? Explain why.

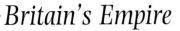

Britain's Empire

Britain had two kinds of empire: countries who depended upon Britain for trade and territories controlled by Britain.

Those countries who depended upon Britain did so for one or more of these reasons:

● Britain was their main customer for raw materials.

● Their trade was carried in British merchant ships.

● They bought British goods because they could not yet make them cheaply enough themselves.

How Britain gained an empire

Britain took control of territories in both an unplanned and planned way.

The discovery of new trade routes by sea instead of overland made it possible for European sea powers like Portugal, the Netherlands, France and Britain to trade directly with India, China, and the islands of the Pacific. Companies like the East India Company set up trading posts on the coasts or by rivers a short distance inland. However, wars with their French rivals in India and quarrels with those who ruled inland led the East India Company to take control of much of India. The expense bankrupted the company. But trade with India was too valuable to lose so from 1783 the government took control of the company. This was an unplanned beginning to British rule of India.

When British explorers discovered territories they had to take them over for the king or queen, even if there were people living there already. To strengthen the claim that these territories belonged to Britain, English men and women arrived to build permanent settlements, called colonies. These planned colonies became a rich source of new trade.

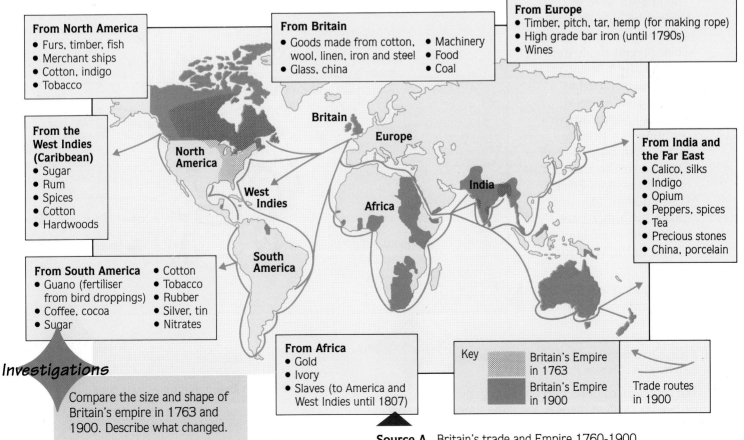

From North America
● Furs, timber, fish
● Merchant ships
● Cotton, indigo
● Tobacco

From Britain
● Goods made from cotton, wool, linen, iron and steel ● Machinery
● Glass, china ● Food
● Coal

From Europe
● Timber, pitch, tar, hemp (for making rope)
● High grade bar iron (until 1790s)
● Wines

From the West Indies (Caribbean)
● Sugar
● Rum
● Spices
● Cotton
● Hardwoods

From India and the Far East
● Calico, silks
● Indigo
● Opium
● Peppers, spices
● Tea
● Precious stones
● China, porcelain

From South America
● Guano (fertiliser from bird droppings)
● Coffee, cocoa
● Sugar
● Cotton
● Tobacco
● Rubber
● Silver, tin
● Nitrates

From Africa
● Gold
● Ivory
● Slaves (to America and West Indies until 1807)

Key
Britain's Empire in 1763
Britain's Empire in 1900
Trade routes in 1900

Source A Britain's trade and Empire 1760–1900

Investigations

Compare the size and shape of Britain's empire in 1763 and 1900. Describe what changed.

21

Britain's colonies in North America

What did the colonies have in common?

The 13 British colonies of North America had only one thing in common: the king of England claimed they belonged to him. Those who settled there were a mixture of families who wanted to escape religious or political persecution, traders and adventurers. Businessmen set up two colonies, Virginia and Massachusetts, as royal charter companies on condition they made a profit. They were 13 separate colonies who each governed themselves differently. They specialised in different ways of making a living: fishing; farming rice, indigo (blue dye), tobacco and sugar. They did not all share the same beliefs and customs. To most colonials a visit to another colony would have been like visiting a foreign country.

How did Britain become more involved in North America?

The English were by no means the only European settlers in North America. Their biggest rivals were the French. A Seven Years War which started in Europe in 1756 soon spread to North America resulting in a British victory. Britain gained all of Canada, vast territories east of the Mississippi River, West and East Florida (taken by France from Spain) and some important islands in the West Indies.

What caused the colonies to unite against Britain?

Britain tried to stop the colonists spreading westwards into American Indian lands and to force them to pay taxes to help cover the costs of governing the colonies in North America. In 1776 the colonies united in a revolution against Britain to fight for their independence.

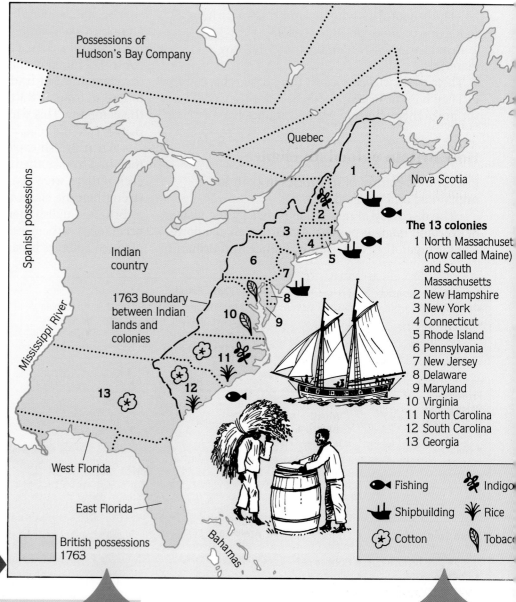

Source B British territories in North America in 1763

The 13 colonies
1 North Massachuset (now called Maine) and South Massachusetts
2 New Hampshire
3 New York
4 Connecticut
5 Rhode Island
6 Pennsylvania
7 New Jersey
8 Delaware
9 Maryland
10 Virginia
11 North Carolina
12 South Carolina
13 Georgia

Fishing Indigo Shipbuilding Rice Cotton Tobacc

Remember...

- Britain had two kinds of empire: a trading empire and colonies.

- The American colonies only united together when Britain upset all of them at the same time. This made them want to be free from British rule.

Investigations

Look at Source **B**. What did Britain stand to lose if the 13 American colonies won their independence?

Captain Cook's voyages

Why was Captain Cook sent to explore the Pacific Ocean?

Cook's mission

In 1767 the Royal Navy chose James Cook (1728-1779) for an important and dangerous mission in the South Pacific.

There were two purposes of the mission: one was scientific; the other secret. The scientists who travelled with him were astronomers and naturalists from the Royal Society. They wanted to observe the passing of the planet Venus between the sun and the earth on 3 June 1769 and to discover new animals and plants. The secret mission was to discover if another continent existed to the south of America and Africa and to take over any territories they found before the French did.

Why was James Cook chosen?

His exceptional ability as a navigator and map maker, rather than his backround or rank, qualified James Cook for the mission to the Pacific. He was the son of a farm labourer who had joined the Royal Navy after turning down the job of commanding a ship which carried coal in the merchant navy. His charts of a difficult section of the St Lawrence River helped British troops reach Quebec in 1759 where they ended French power in North America. The Admiralty promoted Cook only to the rank of lieutenant. Lack of the 'right connections' and snobbery prevented him from reaching the rank of captain until after a second voyage of exploration (1772-5) had made him more famous.

Was Cook's mission a success?

Cook returned to Britain in 1771.
- The observation of the passing of the planet Venus had been unsuccessful because the equipment was not good enough.
- The naturalists were thrilled. One of them, Joseph Banks, had paid £10 000 to go on the voyage. He returned with enough plant specimens and drawings to make himself famous.
- Artists came back with wonderful paintings of what they had seen.

- Cook failed to find a southern continent but mapped and annexed Australia, New Zealand and many Pacific islands as British possessions.
- No one died of scurvy (see Source **B**).

Did Cook's second mission achieve more?

On a second voyage (1772-5), Cook sailed further south than anyone had ever done before. Though he reached the Antarctic Circle he just missed Antarctica and so failed to prove the existence of a southern continent. Nevertheless, the distance covered and the remarkable maps Cook produced of the islands and coasts he explored made this voyage one of the greatest voyages of exploration in history.

Why did the third mission end in tragedy?

The Admiralty tempted Cook into a third voyage (1776-9) to help discover a North West Passage around North America through the Bering Straits. It ended tragically on the island of Hawaii on 14 February 1779. Cook quarrelled with some islanders who hacked him to death. It was a terrible end, but perhaps not a surprising one, to a remarkable man.

Britain's invasion of Australia followed 18 years after Cook first landed in Botany Bay. A fleet of 11 ships arrived there on 26 January 1788. They carried 1030 people who included 548 male and 188 female convicts.

Source A Cook's description of the way he took possession of the lands he discovered for Britain

We enter their ports and attempt to land in a peaceable manner. If this succeeds, all is well, if not we land nevertheless and maintain our footing by the superiority of firearms. In what light can they first look upon us but as invaders of their country?

July 1774

Source B The problems and dangers on Cook's voyages

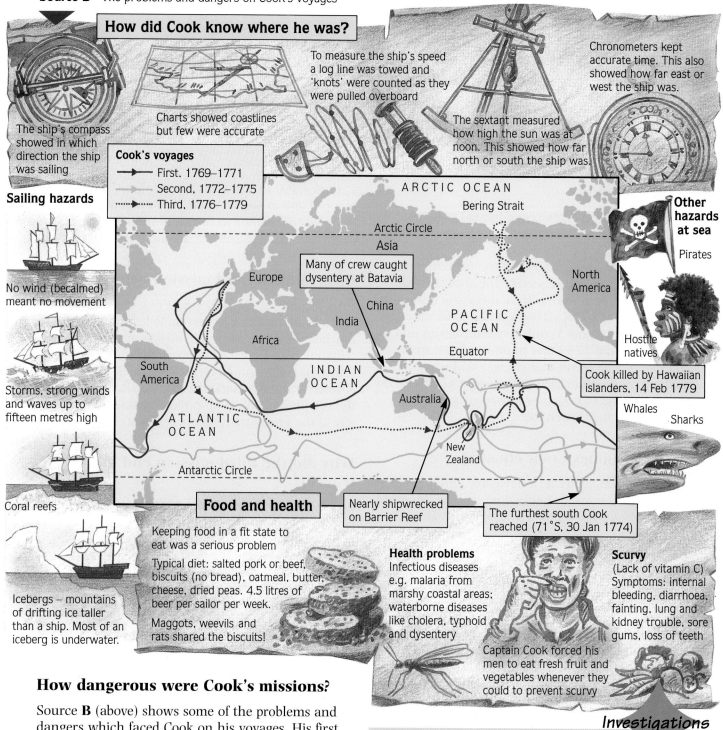

How did Cook know where he was?

Chronometers kept accurate time. This also showed how far east or west the ship was.

The ship's compass showed in which direction the ship was sailing

Charts showed coastlines but few were accurate

To measure the ship's speed a log line was towed and 'knots' were counted as they were pulled overboard

The sextant measured how high the sun was at noon. This showed how far north or south the ship was.

Cook's voyages
→ First, 1769–1771
→ Second, 1772–1775
→ Third, 1776–1779

Sailing hazards

No wind (becalmed) meant no movement

Storms, strong winds and waves up to fifteen metres high

Coral reefs

Icebergs – mountains of drifting ice taller than a ship. Most of an iceberg is underwater.

ARCTIC OCEAN
Bering Strait
Arctic Circle
Asia
Europe
China
India
Africa
Equator
PACIFIC OCEAN
North America
South America
ATLANTIC OCEAN
INDIAN OCEAN
Australia
New Zealand
Antarctic Circle

Many of crew caught dysentery at Batavia

Other hazards at sea
Pirates
Hostile natives
Whales
Sharks

Cook killed by Hawaiian islanders, 14 Feb 1779

Nearly shipwrecked on Barrier Reef

The furthest south Cook reached (71°S, 30 Jan 1774)

Food and health

Keeping food in a fit state to eat was a serious problem

Typical diet: salted pork or beef, biscuits (no bread), oatmeal, butter, cheese, dried peas. 4.5 litres of beer per sailor per week.

Maggots, weevils and rats shared the biscuits!

Health problems
Infectious diseases e.g. malaria from marshy coastal areas; waterborne diseases like cholera, typhoid and dysentery

Captain Cook forced his men to eat fresh fruit and vegetables whenever they could to prevent scurvy

Scurvy
(Lack of vitamin C) Symptoms: internal bleeding, diarrhoea, fainting, lung and kidney trouble, sore gums, loss of teeth

How dangerous were Cook's missions?

Source **B** (above) shows some of the problems and dangers which faced Cook on his voyages. His first ship, the *Endeavour*, was a converted coal ship. It had to be big enough to carry scientific equipment as well as enough supplies for a long voyage. These included animals for fresh eggs, milk and meat, and pickled vegetables, like sauerkraut, which contained vitamin C to prevent scurvy.

Remember...

- Cook's voyages added more territories to the British Empire than any war in Britain's history.

Investigations

1 How did each of the following help Cook work out his ship's position and course: a compass, a sextant, a log line and charts?

2 Which of the hazards and dangers shown in Source **B** did Cook survive?

3 Why is the way Cook died 'perhaps not surprising'?

4 What of importance to Britain was achieved by Cook's voyages of exploration?

5 Suggest reasons why convicted criminals in Britain dreaded transportation to Australia as a punishment.

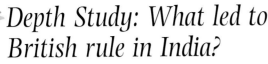

Depth Study: What led to British rule in India?

How did Britain become involved in India?

Trade with the East

In 1600 a powerful Muslim family called the Great Moguls ruled most of India where the majority of people were Hindus.

They allowed the Christian Portuguese, Dutch and English merchants to build trading stations called factories on the coast but not inland. The East India Company's three main trading posts in Bombay, Madras and Calcutta became centres for Britain's Far East trade: spices and peppers from Indonesia; tea from China; cotton, silks, opium and indigo from India. It was not wise to upset the Moguls.

Source A A symbolic painting to show the importance of the Great Mogul, Jahangir. The sunburst is a symbol of royalty. The book being passed to the mullah is probably the **Koran**. Below him are the Sultan of Turkey and King James I of England (1603-25). The hourglass suggests he knows he is human and will not live for ever

Source B Advice given to the East India Company by one of the few Englishmen allowed to meet one of the Moguls

> It is the beggaring of Portugal...It hath been also the error of the Dutch, who seek plantation here by the sword...Let this be received as a rule, that, if you will profit, seek it at sea, and in quiet trade; for without controversy it is an error to affect garrisons and land wars in India.
>
> **The Embassy of Sir Thomas Roe to India 1615-19**

The East India Company followed this advice until 1740 by which time the Great Moguls were no longer strong rulers. By now ministers of the Mogul, generals and **nawabs** began to rule regions such as Hyderabad, Bengal and Oudh like independent princes. Quarrels and family feuds allowed rebels and outsiders, like the Shah of Persia, the Afghans and the Europeans, to take advantage. The East India Company's most serious European rival was now the French India Company. Both

British and French factories were now large fortified settlements defended by European soldiers and Indian soldiers under European command.

How did British power grow?

In a struggle for survival during the European wars (1744-8 and 1756-60) the French India Company and the British East India Company made use of the nawabs and their armies to fight each other. British victories over the French and the nawabs left the East India Company in control of much of India (see Source **C**, page 26).

Many of those who worked for the East India Company returned to England fabulously rich from plunder, private trading, and by accepting presents given as bribes by wealthy Indians. These 'nabobs', as they were nicknamed, used their wealth to buy huge estates, build wonderful homes and buy their way into Parliament. The most famous of these was Robert Clive.

Key words

Koran The sacred book of Islam containing the words of Mohammed.
Nawab A local governor.

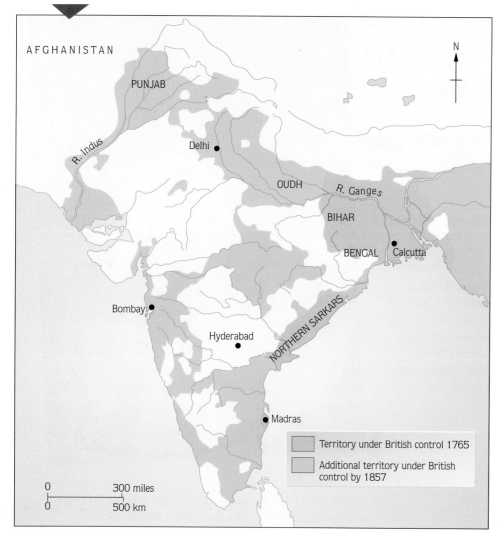

AFGHANISTAN

PUNJAB

R. Indus

Delhi

OUDH

R. Ganges

BIHAR

BENGAL   Calcutta

Bombay

NORTHERN SARKARS

Hyderabad

Madras

Territory under British control 1765

Additional territory under British control by 1857

0   300 miles
0   500 km

What did Robert Clive achieve in India?

In 1744 Robert Clive (1724–74) started work in Madras for the East India Company after a sea journey from London which lasted nearly 15 months. His job as a clerk earned him a salary of £5 a year. War with France gave Clive the chance to give up this dull job to become a soldier for the Company and then steward responsible for supplies to the European troops at Madras. He returned to England in 1743 a hero, with a wife and a fortune of £40 000 in profits made from the supplies to the fort.

He stayed in England long enough to pay off debts on his family's estate in Shropshire, buy a house for himself and his parents in London, and waste the rest of his fortune in a failed attempt to get into Parliament. Then in 1755 the East India Company persuaded him to return to India as a lieutenant colonel to deal with more trouble from the French. He took with him his wife, Margaret, but left their one-year-old son in England.

By the time Clive returned to England again in 1760 he had taken control of the whole of Bengal for the East India Company, made a personal fortune of £243 000 and had persuaded the Mogul Emperor to grant him a jagir (land taxes worth £30 000 a year for life).

The key to his success was to persuade the nawab of Bengal's army commander, Mir Jaffar, to desert his master in the middle of a battle at Plassey in 1757. He did so by making a treaty with a forged signature of a representative of the British government. This promised to back Mir Jaffar as the new nawab.

Source E   Robert Clive's letter to the prime minister, William Pitt, 7 January 1759. Clive suggests that the new territories in India were too big for the East India Company to rule and that direct control by the British company could be bought

Source D
One of Robert Clive's country homes: Claremont in Surrey

So large a **sovereignty** may possibly be an object too extensive for a mercantile company; it is to be feared they are not of themselves able, without the nation's assistance, to maintain so wide a dominion...there will be little or no difficulty in obtaining the absolute possession of these rich kingdoms; and this with the Moghul's own consent, on condition of paying him less than a fifth of the **revenues** thereof...it is well worth consideration that this project may be brought about without draining the mother country, as has been much the case with our possessions in America.

Corruption and greed now threatened to bankrupt the East India Company. Clive returned again to India in 1765 to reorganise the way the company behaved in Bengal and to put an end to the system of rewards and bribes which had made him and others rich. Clive made a deal with the Mogul Emperor, Shah Alam. In exchange for protection from his enemies the Mogul Emperor now recognised the East India Company's authority in Bengal by granting it the power (diwani) to collect taxes in Bengal (Source **F**).

Overwork and stress led Clive to a nervous breakdown and his return to Britain in 1767.

Robert Clive was now a knight, an Irish lord and a wealthy landowner with three country estates, a town house in London and a house in Bath. Such wealth led to jealousy and suspicion.

In 1770 a terrible famine in Bengal and Bihar killed over a third of the population. Enemies in the East India Company and Parliament stirred up criticism of how Clive had made his fortune.

Source G   Clive's defence of his behaviour in India

> A great prince was dependent on my pleasure, an **opulent** city lay at my mercy; its richest bankers bid against each other for my smiles. I walked through vaults which were thrown open to me alone, piled on either side with gold and jewels! Mr Chairman, at this moment, I stand astonished at my own moderation.
>
> **From the report of a Committee of Enquiry, 1772**

Clive was a depressed and ill man. He often took large doses of opium to dull the pain of stomach cramps, gallstones and gout. He died on 22 November 1774. His family said he took an overdose of opium by accident but it was rumoured he cut his throat.

How did the British government become more involved?

The East India Company was losing money and struggled to govern the territories it controlled. From 1773 the British government stepped in. It appointed a Governor General to rule the East India

Source F   The Mogul Emperor Shah Alam granting the diwani of Bengal to Robert Clive. This event really took place inside a tent where the Emperor's throne was placed on a table

Company's territories and backed the conquest of the rest of India. The British introduced new methods of collecting taxes and built colleges to train civil servants to govern the territories. In 1857 a mutiny of Indian soldiers in the army developed into a serious rebellion by the landlords of Oudh and some Indian princes. Once this was crushed the British government took over from the East India Company and became the ruler of India.

Remember...

- **British power in India started with trade.**
- **Robert Clive won control of Bengal for the East India Company.**
- **The British government backed the conquest of the rest of India.**

Investigations

1 Compare Sources **A** and **F**. How do they show that the power of the Mogul Emperors and the British in India changed?

2 How did each of the following cause the British to become involved in India:
   a) trade   **b)** war   **c)** Robert Clive?

3 Read Source **E**.
   a) Why did Robert Clive think that the British government could rule India more easily than the East India Company?
   b) How did he think that the Mogul Emperor could be persuaded to give up his power to the British?
   c) What advantage did he think the rule of India would have over the rule of the American colonies?

4 Suggest what Robert Clive's critics would have thought of his answer to them in Source **G**?

Key words

Opulent Rich • **Revenues** Taxes
Sovereignty Kingdom

4 Rule Britannia

Did losing the American colonies matter?

> **What was the impact on Britain of the American War of Independence and the French Revolution?**

In 1775 the 13 American colonies united together to fight Britain and in 1776 they declared their independence.

Source A Declaration of Independence

> **G**overnments are instituted among Men, deriving their just powers from the consent of the governed. That whenever any Form of Government becomes destructive of these ends, it is the Right of the People to alter or to abolish it and to institute new government.

Source B John Wilkes' speech in the House of Commons following the rebels' victory over the British army at Saratoga in 1777

> **I** am sorry that 800 valiant English and Germans [German soldiers hired by the British government] were killed in a bad cause, in fighting the best **constitution** on earth.

What was at stake for Britain?

The loss of the colonies would affect Britain's relationships and trade with other countries. It could affect:
- Britain's enemies – countries like France saw opportunities for revenge after losing wars against Britain in North America and India. They wanted to isolate and weaken Britain.
- British trade – the 13 colonies took 20 per cent of all British exports and supplied 30 per cent of all British imports.
- The United Kingdom – the British government feared that the Scots, Irish and Welsh might try to follow the example of the American colonists and rebel.

Source C A cartoon criticising the actions of the British government against the colonies

- Political change in Britain – the ideas about government in the rebels' *Declaration of Independence* might inspire rebellion in Britain.

What were the consequences for Britain?

- Britain was defeated in 1783 by the rebels helped by France, Spain and Holland.
- The **national debt** increased from £138 000 000 to £249 000 000.
- British trade flourished. The United States of America was Britain's most important source of raw cotton. By 1800 the USA took one quarter of all British exports.
- The risk of another rebellion closer to Britain in 1782 forced the government to give Irish Protestants more control over their own affairs. Many Scots used the opportunity to win favour by showing support for Britain (Source **C**).
- Even some senior British politicians sympathised with the rebels. William Pitt believed they had been treated unfairly and that the war was a mistake.

Investigations

1 Look at Sources **A** and **B**. Why do you think John Wilkes thought that the American rebels had the 'best constitution on earth'?

2 Look at Source **C**.
   a) Who do you think the goose represents?
   b) Who in the United Kingdom does the cartoon suggest supported the British government against the American colonies?

3 With a partner, work out the arguments **for** and **against** the view that 'The loss of the American colonies was a disaster for Britain'.

Key words
Constitution The rules of government.
National debt Money owed which was borrowed by the government.

War with France

The French Revolution

In 1789 millions of French people took part in a revolution to get rid of an unpopular king and an old system of government. They looked forward to a better life under a new system of government called a 'republic' which means 'rule by the people'.

At first many Britons thought what had happened in France was wonderful – famous poets like William Wordsworth and William Blake wrote poems to celebrate. People formed corresponding societies and exchanged letters with revolutionaries. However, by 1792 excitement had turned to terror. Revolutionaries broke into the prisons of Paris and murdered 1400 prisoners suspected of being supporters of King Louis XVI. Cartoons like Source **A** show the horror that many British people felt.

Source A A cartoon by James Gillray commenting on the massacres by revolutionaries in France in 1792

29

The French government now called for worldwide revolution. Their slogan was 'Liberty, equality and **fraternity**'. Britain allied with Austria and Prussia and went to war with France in 1793 to stop the revolution from spreading. War with France lasted until 1815, with temporary peace between 1802–5 and in 1814.

Danger from within Britain

To prevent revolution starting in Britain, the government passed laws so that:
- suspects could be arrested without evidence and held in prison without trial.
- no foreigner could enter the country without special permission.
- no more than 50 people could meet together to protest against the government.

However, hunger in 1795 led to bread riots and after George III was attacked on his way to open Parliament it became an act of **treason** to encourage violence against the king. More serious were mutinies by sailors in the Royal Navy at Nore and Spithead in 1787. As a result in 1799–1800 the government banned any kind of **combination** or trade union.

Threat of invasion

Fear of invasion by the French led to a system of fortifications being built along the coasts of Britain and the Channel Islands. These included small circular forts with thick walls, called Martello towers. When Irish rebels tried to help the French land an invasion force in Ireland in 1798 the government decided the time had come to take stronger control of Ireland. In 1800 an Act of Union replaced the Irish Parliament with direct rule from the British Parliament.

Turning points in the wars with France

1799
- The French found a new leader, a brilliant soldier called Napoleon Bonaparte.
- The battle of the Nile in Egypt – the British Navy led by Horatio Nelson put a stop to Napoleon's plans to conquer the Middle East.

1805
- The battle of Trafalgar, off the south coast of Spain. Nelson's defeat of the French navy saved Britain from invasion and cost him his life.

1806
- Napoleon, who described Britain as 'a nation of shopkeepers', believed he could starve Britain into defeat by preventing the continent of Europe trading with Britain. Portugal refused to support this plan from the start. In 1810 Russia withdrew its support and the plan failed.

1808–13
- The British Army, led by Sir Arthur Wellesley (the Duke of Wellington from 1809) helped the Portuguese and Spanish drive the French out of Portugal and Spain.

1815
- The battle of Waterloo. After a temporary defeat and exile in 1814 Napoleon made a dramatic comeback. A final showdown took place at Waterloo in Belgium. There the British army, led by the Duke of Wellington, and helped by Belgians, Dutch, Germans and Prussians, won a decisive victory over Napoleon which ended the war.

Key words

Combination People uniting to take action against authority or employers.
Fraternity Friendship in support of liberty and equality.

Treason The action of an enemy of the country punishable by death.

JOHN BULL. Happy.

JOHN BULL, going to the WARS.

JOHN BULL'S Property in danger.

JOHN BULL'S glorious Return.

JOHN BULL'S PROGRESS.

Remember...

- The American War of Independence and French Revolution caused both hopes and fears of political change in Britain.

- Defeat in 1783 weakened Britain as a world power. Victory over France in 1815 restored Britain as a world power.

- Keys to Britain's survival were a healthy economy and decisive battles won by Nelson and Wellington.

The cost of war

As Source **B** suggests, war with France caused mixed reactions even in 1793. By 1815 the national debt had risen to £834 000 000.

Investigations

1 Who does John Bull represent in Source **B**?

2 Describe how James Gilray felt about
   a) events in France in 1792 (Source **A**, page 29)
   b) going to war with France in 1793 (Source **B**).

Depth Study: Nelson's navy and Wellington's army

How did Nelson and his navy compare with Wellington and his army?

Man-of-war

Britain's sea power depended on a fleet of large wooden ships called men-of-war. A single man-of-war needed a crew of up to 800 men including officers, ordinary seamen, and marines (Source **A**).

Conditions were crowded and unpleasant. Discipline was severe and the food often revolting. Many sailors were forced into the navy by **press gangs**, including Tobias Smollett (Source **B**).

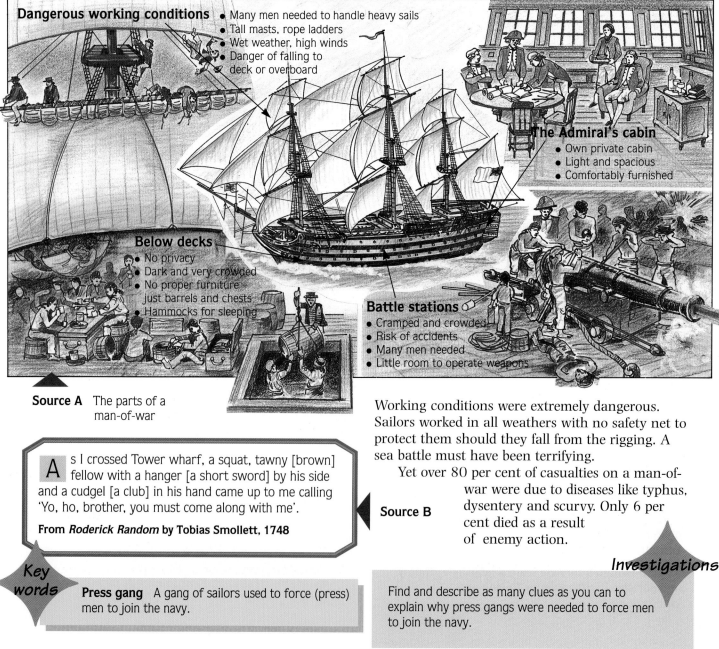

Dangerous working conditions
- Many men needed to handle heavy sails
- Tall masts, rope ladders
- Wet weather, high winds
- Danger of falling to deck or overboard

The Admiral's cabin
- Own private cabin
- Light and spacious
- Comfortably furnished

Below decks
- No privacy
- Dark and very crowded
- No proper furniture just barrels and chests
- Hammocks for sleeping

Battle stations
- Cramped and crowded
- Risk of accidents
- Many men needed
- Little room to operate weapons

Source A The parts of a man-of-war

> A s I crossed Tower wharf, a squat, tawny [brown] fellow with a hanger [a short sword] by his side and a cudgel [a club] in his hand came up to me calling 'Yo, ho, brother, you must come along with me'.
>
> **From *Roderick Random* by Tobias Smollett, 1748**

Source B

Working conditions were extremely dangerous. Sailors worked in all weathers with no safety net to protect them should they fall from the rigging. A sea battle must have been terrifying.

Yet over 80 per cent of casualties on a man-of-war were due to diseases like typhus, dysentery and scurvy. Only 6 per cent died as a result of enemy action.

Key words

Press gang A gang of sailors used to force (press) men to join the navy.

Investigations

Find and describe as many clues as you can to explain why press gangs were needed to force men to join the navy.

A soldier's life

Source C
By the Duke of Wellington in 1813

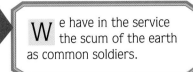

We have in the service the scum of the earth as common soldiers.

Few men joined the army just for adventure. Many became soldiers to escape poverty or being sent to prison for debt, theft or violent crime. A number of recruits had drink problems or were escaping from trouble at home. Some were mentally deranged and excited by violence.

In the 1790s the pay was 1 shilling (5p) a day. A bricklayer earned nearly four times as much. Bread was free but a soldier had to buy the rest of his food. There are stories of soldiers crying from hunger in their bunks at night. A common reason for desertion was starvation.

Source E A flogging on the triangle in 1822

Home leave was usually at the end of a tour of duty or a campaign. Even then families were often too far away to be visited. Some soldiers were away from home for as long as 16 years. However, the army allowed a limited number of wives to travel with their husbands on active service. These women helped to look after the wounded (Source **D**).

Source D A cartoon of the British Army on the march at the time of the Napoleonic wars

To keep discipline the army relied on flogging. In one typical case a soldier who fell asleep on guard duty received 229 lashes. He died eight days later after the wounds on his back turned septic. In 1815 sentences of 1000 lashes were given for robbery.

Officers
A man wanting promotion to a higher rank depended on his having money and influence rather than quality, skill or qualifications (Source **F**).

Source F By the Duke of York's Adjutant-General

His friends (i.e. family) can give him a thousand pounds with which to go to the auction rooms in Charles Street and in a fortnight he becomes a captain. Out of fifteen regiments of cavalry and twenty-six of infantry which we have, twenty-one are commanded literally by boys or idiots.

Investigations

1 How do you explain
   a) Wellington's opinion of soldiers in the British Army (Source **C**)?
   b) the opinion of officers given in Source **F**?

2 What is the artist's message about the British Army in Source **D**?

3 Why do you think severe punishments of soldiers were thought necessary?

Nelson at Trafalgar

Napoleon planned to invade England. Nelson's job was to stop this from happening. In October 1805 Nelson deliberately allowed 33 French and Spanish ships to leave Cadiz harbour because he wanted to destroy them in a battle at sea. On 21 October 1805 Nelson attacked them at Cape Trafalgar.

To prepare for a battle, days at sea were spent practising, keeping the men fit, and making sure his officers knew exactly what to do. The last thing he did personally was to write a will for Emma Hamilton, his mistress, and their daughter and pray for victory.

Nelson's tactics

Nelson did not follow the usual tactics of bringing his ships in a line alongside the enemy. Instead, he approached bow first in two columns, aiming to split up the enemy line (Source **G**). As his ships' guns could only fire sideways, this meant they could not respond to enemy fire until they crossed the enemy line.

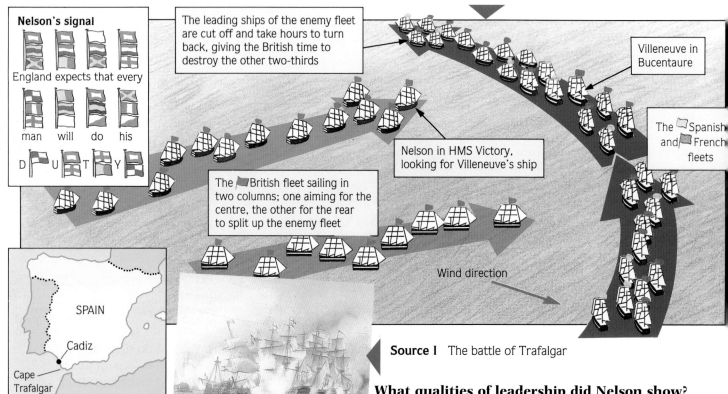

Source G The plan of the battle of Trafalgar

Nelson's signal

England expects that every

man will do his

D U T Y

The leading ships of the enemy fleet are cut off and take hours to turn back, giving the British time to destroy the other two-thirds

Villeneuve in Bucentaure

The Spanish and French fleets

Nelson in HMS Victory, looking for Villeneuve's ship

The British fleet sailing in two columns; one aiming for the centre, the other for the rear to split up the enemy fleet

Wind direction

SPAIN

Cadiz

Cape Trafalgar

Source I The battle of Trafalgar

Source H A description of the battle by a Royal Marine on HMS *Victory*

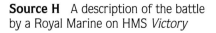

We were engaging on both sides; every gun was going off…recoiling with violence, reports louder than thunder, the decks heaving and the sides straining…Lips might move, but orders and hearing were out of the question; everything was done by signs.

What qualities of leadership did Nelson show?

Nelson inspired his men by leading from the front and searching for the French Admiral, Villeneuve, hoping to fight ship to ship. He made sure his men could see him on deck despite the risk of being an obvious target for enemy snipers.

A sniper's bullet hit Nelson in his left shoulder. Nelson felt it break his backbone. He lived long enough to know he had won the battle of Trafalgar. His body was first preserved in a cask of brandy then spirits of wine while waiting for burial in St Paul's Cathedral in London.

Remember…

- **Victory at Trafalgar ended France's hopes of invasion.**

- **It gave the Royal Navy control of the seas. This made possible the growth of Britain's empire.**

Investigations

1 a) What were the risks of Nelson's plan of attack shown in Source **G**?
  b) Why do you think the plan was successful?

2 Why are Sources **H** and **I** both helpful and unhelpful as evidence to historians?

Wellington at Waterloo

On 18 June 1815 Napoleon attacked Wellington's army at Waterloo, 11 miles south of Brussels in Belgium. Victory for Napoleon would mean a remarkable comeback after losing power in 1814. His success depended on defeating Wellington before Britain's allies, the Prussians led by Blücher, arrived.

Napoleon's tactics were to launch a 'dummy' attack against the enemies' right to draw off troops from Wellington's centre where he would launch the real attack with large numbers.

Wellington used defensive tactics perfected in his campaigns in India and against Napoleon's army in Portugal and Spain.

What did the soldiers experience?
Rain made fighting conditions extremely muddy and wet.

What qualities of leadership did Wellington show?
Throughout the battle Wellington took personal risks, galloping his horse, Copenhagen, everywhere to give orders and encouragement. Despite several narrow escapes he showed a steady nerve. The Prussians arrived just in time.

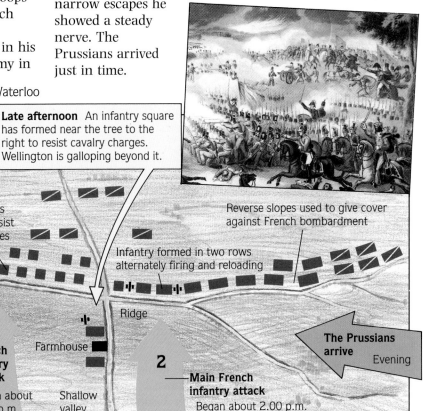

Source J The battle of Waterloo

London
Brussels
Waterloo
FRANCE

Late afternoon An infantry square has formed near the tree to the right to resist cavalry charges. Wellington is galloping beyond it.

Positions near roads helped rapid movement of troops and horse artillery

Infantry forms squares to resist cavalry charges

Reverse slopes used to give cover against French bombardment

Infantry formed in two rows alternately firing and reloading

Ridge

Ridge

Farmhouse

The Prussians arrive   Evening

Chateau

1
'Dummy' attack to cause a diversion. Began 11.35 a.m.

4
Imperial Guard attack   Evening

3
French cavalry attack
Began about 4.00 p.m.

Shallow valley

2
Main French infantry attack
Began about 2.00 p.m. after bombardment by cannons lasting 30 minutes

KEY Wellington's army; British (24,000), Belgian, Dutch and German troops. Total: 67,661 men, 156 big guns

Napoleon's army 71,947 men 246 big guns

Infantry   Cavalry

Artillery (big guns)

Prussian army

Casualties (dead or wounded)
Wellington's army   15,000
Prussian army   7,000
Napoleon's army   25,000
Horses   10,000 (out of 30,000)

Source K Sergeant Wheeler's description of enemy cavalry charge

We saw them coming and was prepared, we opened fire, the work was done in an instant…I…never before beheld such a sight…as about an hundred men and horses could be huddled together where they lay. Those who were shot dead were fortunate for the wounded horses in their struggles by plunging and kicking so finished what we had begun.

Remember…

- **Wellington's victory at Waterloo ended Napoleon's career and led to peace with France.**

Investigations

1 Study Source **J**.
   a) In what ways were Wellington's tactics different from Napoleon's?
   b) Why do you think Wellington chose these tactics?

2 Wellington later described the battle of Waterloo as 'the nearest run thing you ever saw in your life'. Which of Sources **J** and **K** best help to explain this description and why?

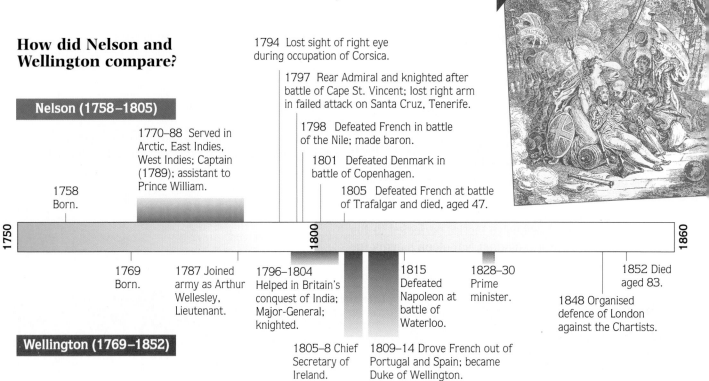

How did Nelson and Wellington compare?

Nelson (1758–1805)

1758 Born.

1770–88 Served in Arctic, East Indies, West Indies; Captain (1789); assistant to Prince William.

1794 Lost sight of right eye during occupation of Corsica.

1797 Rear Admiral and knighted after battle of Cape St. Vincent; lost right arm in failed attack on Santa Cruz, Tenerife.

1798 Defeated French in battle of the Nile; made baron.

1801 Defeated Denmark in battle of Copenhagen.

1805 Defeated French at battle of Trafalgar and died, aged 47.

1750 ... **1800** ... **1860**

1769 Born.

1787 Joined army as Arthur Wellesley, Lieutenant.

1796–1804 Helped in Britain's conquest of India; Major-General; knighted.

1805–8 Chief Secretary of Ireland.

1809–14 Drove French out of Portugal and Spain; became Duke of Wellington.

1815 Defeated Napoleon at battle of Waterloo.

1828–30 Prime minister.

1848 Organised defence of London against the Chartists.

1852 Died aged 83.

Wellington (1769–1852)

What did Nelson and Wellington have in common?

● Both men became friends with members of the royal family. Prince William (the future King William IV) gave away the bride away at Nelson's wedding and Wellington was godfather to Queen Victoria's son who was named Arthur in his honour.

● Both men became officers and achieved promotion through family influence.

● They inspired confidence even among the lowest ranks.

● Before a battle they prepared carefully and during a battle they took personal risks.

● In their personal lives they both treated their wives unkindly and were attracted to other women.

How were they different?

● Nelson's father was a vicar of Burnham Thorpe in Norfolk. Wellington's father was a lord with an estate in Ireland.

● Nelson lived to the age of 47 and died in battle. Wellington lived to the age of 83 and died at home sitting in his favourite chair.

● Nelson went to sea at the age of 12. Though he spoke in Parliament after becoming a lord he did not have a career in politics. Wellington achieved fame both as a soldier and politician. He joined the army at the age of 18. In 1828 he became prime minister.

● Nelson was vain and enjoyed publicity. Though he was strict on discipline ordinary sailors remembered him for his fairness, his ability to talk easily to them and for acts of kindness. The fact that he lost an eye and an arm and even died in action made him more of a hero. His very public affair with a married woman, Lady Emma Hamilton, did not harm his reputation.

● Wellington's support for the right of Roman Catholics to become MPs and his opposition to a fairer system of elections made him an unpopular politician. Soldiers remembered Wellington as a 'keen flogger' but respected him. He disliked publicity. He had an abrupt manner of speaking but a good sense of humour.

Remember...

● Nelson and Wellington won decisive battles which saved their country from defeat by France.

Investigations

1 Why do you think Source **L** shows Emma Hamilton, Prince William and George III who were not really present at Nelson's death?

2 What were the strengths and weaknesses of Nelson and Wellington?

3 Why do you think Nelson was more popular with the public than Wellington?

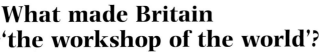

5 What made Britain 'the workshop of the world'?

Farming

Introduction

By 1838 the politician, Disraeli, was able to describe Britain as 'the workshop of the world'. This chapter investigates the changes which made this transformation possible.

Why were there changes in farming?

Wealthy landowners

By 1873 7000 landowners out of a population of 32 million owned 80 per cent of the land in the United Kingdom. Only wealthy landowners could afford the expense of enclosing land and the risk of experimenting with new methods (Source **B**).

Better communication

Experts like Jethro Tull and Arthur Young spread ideas in books and journals. King George III wrote articles in *Farmers* magazine using the name Ralph Robinson and made new methods well known by using them on his farm at Windsor. Farmers formed agricultural societies which sponsored shows to look at new breeds of animals and new machines for sowing, harvesting and **threshing**.

The French Wars 1793–1815

By 1793 most bread in Britain was made with wheat. From 1806 Napoleon tried to starve Britain into surrender by blocking trade with the continent. This made it more difficult to import wheat from Poland and East Prussia. Wheat prices more than doubled. Landowners made a lot of money by clearing more land for growing **corn**.

Falling prices and foreign competition

Farmers converted too much land to growing crops. Overproduction led to a fall in the price of corn and loss of profits. A series of wet seasons and poor harvests put up costs. Landowners, who controlled Parliament, passed a Corn Law in 1815 to prevent imports of foreign corn below certain prices. This made food more expensive. A campaign against the unfairness of the Corn Law and a famine in Ireland led to its removal in 1846. To

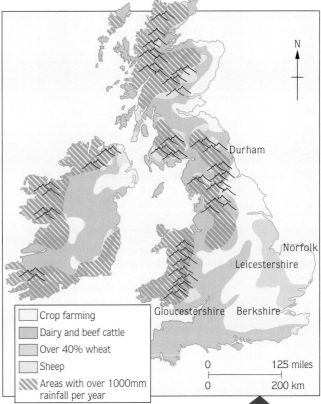

Source A The main farming areas of Britain in 1900. Different kinds of farming suit different kinds of land, soil and climate.

survive competition from cheaper foreign corn British farmers either had to become better farmers or reduce costs by using machines to take the place of farm workers.

Population changes

The growth of the UK population from 9.5 to 41 million by 1901 increased the demand for food.

Railways

From the 1830s railways provided quicker, cheaper transport so that farmers could supply towns from greater distances. By the 1870s, however, railways had spread across North America resulting in more competition from cheaper imported corn.

Investigations

Why was there a greater need to improve farming after the wars with France?

Key words

Threshing Separating grain from the straw.
Corn All kinds of grain crop.

How did farming change?

● **Reclamation** Landowners added 10 per cent to England's crop-growing land by draining marshlands like the Fens in East Anglia and by clearing waste land.
● **Enclosures** Landowners combined strips of land into larger fields and enclosed them with fences, hedges or stone walls. Enclosures began slowly in the 1400s but accelerated in the 1700s.
● **Soil improvement** Wealthy landowners like Viscount 'Turnip' Townshend (1764–1817) and Thomas Coke (1754–1842) encouraged farmers to use up-to-date methods of crop rotation and soil improvement on their estates.

Source B Better use of land

Before
Use of fields rotates
• Farmers had strips of land scattered among the fields
• No fences, hedges or walls to separate fields
• Fields were left fallow (rested) in turn

Wheat
marsh
Fallow (resting) - cattle graze and fertilise with manure
wasteland
Barley
Common land for animals to graze (Only a few animals were kept in winter for breeding- the rest were slaughtered for meat)

After
Use of fields rotates
• Bigger plots of land with more room to turn machines
• A careful rotation of crops looked after the soil and made it unnecessary to 'rest' fields
  Turnips clean the soil (but do not grow well in clay soils)
  Clover restores nitrogen to the soil
• From the 1830s and 1840s farmers used fertilisers like phosphates from Germany and guano (bird droppings) from South America

Turnips
- root crop
- cleans soil
- allows weeding
- winter feed for animals
hedges to separate fields
ditches
Room to turn machines and horses
Barley
Cattle
Sheep
More land for crops and animals
Clover
- restores nitrogen to the soil
- roots break up soil
- winter feed for animals

Source C New machinery

● Jethro Tull (Berkshire; 1674–1741) invented a seed drill and horse-drawn hoe. These were available from the 1730s but did not work on heavy soils.
● The first **threshing** machine was invented in 1786 but it was not until the 1820s and 1830s that there were enough of them to cause alarm to farm workers.
● Widespread introduction of mechanical mowers for hay cutting, and reapers for cutting and binding corn did not happen until the 1850s.

Old method of threshing with flails

A mechanical reaper

Harvest time in Gloucestershire in 1700s

Source D Selective breeding

● By carefully choosing mates for animals it became possible to improve or develop new breeds.
● Robert Bakewell (1725–95) from Leicestershire bred cattle (longhorns) and sheep (New Leicesters) for meat, and new work horses (shires) which replaced oxen for pulling farm machinery.
● The Colling brothers bred Durham shorthorns (cattle) from which dairy shorthorns are descended.
● Joseph Tuley, a Yorkshire weaver, helped to develop the large white pig.

Border Leicester sheep
Dairy shorthorn
Large white pig

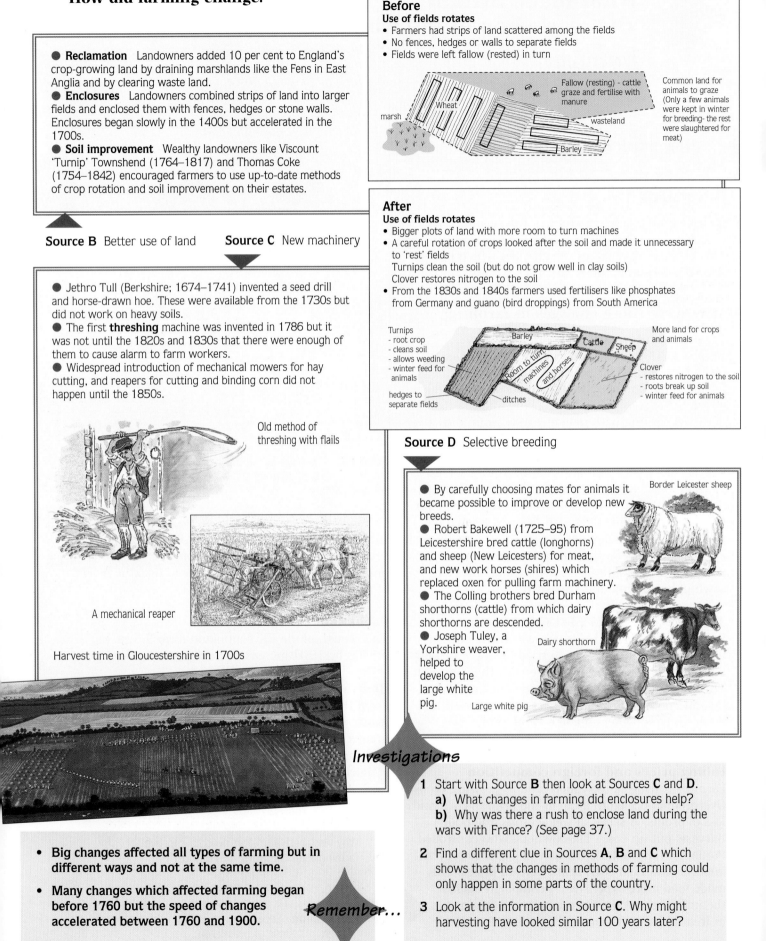

Investigations

1 Start with Source **B** then look at Sources **C** and **D**.
   a) What changes in farming did enclosures help?
   b) Why was there a rush to enclose land during the wars with France? (See page 37.)

2 Find a different clue in Sources **A**, **B** and **C** which shows that the changes in methods of farming could only happen in some parts of the country.

3 Look at the information in Source **C**. Why might harvesting have looked similar 100 years later?

• **Big changes affected all types of farming but in different ways and not at the same time.**

• **Many changes which affected farming began before 1760 but the speed of changes accelerated between 1760 and 1900.**

Remember...

Iron

Why did iron making improve?

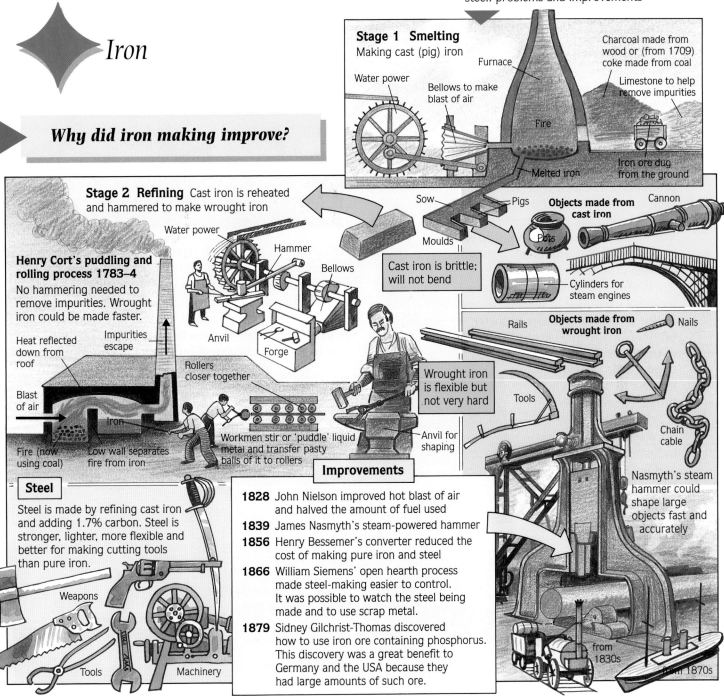

Source A The stages in making iron and steel: problems and improvements

Stage 1 Smelting
Making cast (pig) iron

Water power

Furnace

Charcoal made from wood or (from 1709) coke made from coal

Bellows to make blast of air

Limestone to help remove impurities

Fire

Melted iron

Iron ore dug from the ground

Stage 2 Refining Cast iron is reheated and hammered to make wrought iron

Water power

Hammer

Bellows

Sow

Pigs

Moulds

Objects made from cast iron

Pots

Cannon

Cast iron is brittle; will not bend

Cylinders for steam engines

Henry Cort's puddling and rolling process 1783–4
No hammering needed to remove impurities. Wrought iron could be made faster.

Anvil

Forge

Heat reflected down from roof

Impurities escape

Rollers closer together

Blast of air

Iron

Fire (now using coal)

Low wall separates fire from iron

Workmen stir or 'puddle' liquid metal and transfer pasty balls of it to rollers

Anvil for shaping

Wrought iron is flexible but not very hard

Rails

Objects made from wrought iron

Nails

Tools

Anchor

Chain cable

Nasmyth's steam hammer could shape large objects fast and accurately

Steel

Steel is made by refining cast iron and adding 1.7% carbon. Steel is stronger, lighter, more flexible and better for making cutting tools than pure iron.

Weapons

Tools

Machinery

Improvements

1828 John Nielson improved hot blast of air and halved the amount of fuel used

1839 James Nasmyth's steam-powered hammer

1856 Henry Bessemer's converter reduced the cost of making pure iron and steel

1866 William Siemens' open hearth process made steel-making easier to control. It was possible to watch the steel being made and to use scrap metal.

1879 Sidney Gilchrist-Thomas discovered how to use iron ore containing phosphorus. This discovery was a great benefit to Germany and the USA because they had large amounts of such ore.

from 1830s

from 1870s

A declining industry

In 1750, despite an increasing demand for iron, the British iron industry was in decline. Britain depended on importing wrought iron from Sweden, Russia and the American colonies.

One reason for the decline of the British iron industry in the first part of the eighteenth century was that it depended upon charcoal (made from wood) for smelting. However the government took action to stop the cutting down of forests to make charcoal because timber was needed for the Navy.

In 1709 Abraham Darby I of Coalbrookdale

(1677–1717) discovered a way of using coke (made from coal) instead of charcoal for smelting iron. Later Henry Cort perfected a type of blast furnace which made it possible to use the heat from coal indirectly to smelt iron so that impurities from the coal did not mix with, and spoil, the metal. The result was that iron smelting moved from forest areas like Sussex and the Forest of Dean to the coalfields of South Wales, the Midlands and the North. By coincidence, iron ore was often found near coal mines. The price of iron fell and the demand for iron and steel increased.

Important breakthroughs

Look carefully at Source **B**. It shows men making a very large anchor for a warship in Bristol in 1836. The customer is the ruler of Egypt. Notice the number of men hauling up the huge hammer to drop on to the heated iron on the left to help shape the anchor while the men with hand-held hammers add the finishing touches. To the right two men are making a huge chain cable. This process of making products out of iron is called forging. The iron used here is called wrought iron or bar iron. Not until 1783–4 did Henry Cort make it possible to convert 'pig' or cast iron into wrought iron cheaply enough to make it worth producing wrought iron in Britain in large quantities (Source **A**).

Within less than 100 years the British iron industry expanded to become the greatest producer in the world and a major exporter of iron and products made from iron. Source **C** shows a section of the Great Exhibition at Crystal Palace near London in 1851, which Prince Albert helped to organise to show off the achievements of British industry. Notice the roof and pillars. The Crystal Palace was specially built with glass supported by an iron structure.

An even stronger, lighter and more flexible metal is steel, made from iron mixed with carbon. It was not until processes invented by Henry Bessemer in 1856, William Siemens in 1866 and Sidney Gilchrist-Thomas in 1879 (Source **A**) that Britain became a major steel producer too. However, by this time the USA and Germany were catching up with Britain. In 1900 Germany was exporting iron and steel products to Britain.

Source C
The Machinery Court at the Great Exhibition, 1851

Remember...

Rapid progress in making iron and steel was made possible by four important discoveries:

- The use of coke and then coal to replace charcoal for smelting.
- Henry Cort's puddling and rolling process for making wrought iron.
- Bessemer's converter and Siemens' open hearth process for making steel.

Investigations

1 Study Source **A** (page 39). Prepare a talk lasting two minutes to explain how wrought iron and steel were made. Take it in turns with a partner to practice and listen to each other's talk. Write down at least one thing your partner leaves out or does not make clear.

2 a) Describe the dangers to health and safety shown in Source **B**.
   b) What difference would James Nasymth's steam-powered hammer (Source **A**) have made to this scene?

3 Look at Source **C**. Design a poster to attract people to come and see the Machinery Court at the Great Exhibition in 1851.

Factories

What was new about factories?

The importance of textiles

Making textiles (cloth) was Britain's second biggest industry. Before 1750 most people wore clothes made from wool and **linen**. Only wealthy people could afford cotton cloth. However, cheap raw cotton from America led Britain to make more cotton cloth and to stop importing Indian cottons. Between 1750 and 1850 cotton not only overtook wool as Britain's most valuable textile but became Britain's most valuable single export (Source **B**). This 'take-over' by cotton was an industrial revolution made possible by new technology and factories.

Compare Source **A** with Source **C**. In both scenes yarn, the thread for making the cloth, is being spun. In Source **A** people are working at home spinning flax for linen on spinning wheels. In Source **C** huge machines are mass-producing yarn from cotton.

Spinning and weaving cloth at home was called the domestic system. This system could not supply weavers with cotton yarn of the right quality fast enough.

In 1768 Richard Arkwright produced a spinning machine called the water frame. It was powered by a water wheel and was too big to fit into people's homes. A water wheel (or a steam engine) could power several of these machines working at the same time in one building, called a mill or a factory. Improvements to factory machines soon made it possible to produce yarn for making finer cloth like muslin. It took longer before weaving took place in factories too. However, the demand for uniforms and materials during the French Wars helps to explain why so many factories adopted the power loom for weaving between 1800–12.

A visitor walking around Manchester in 1815 counted over 60 spinning mills in a 15 minute walk. A typical factory or mill in Lancashire was quite small and employed fewer than 100 workers. However, there were some huge factories built with four or five storeys. Workers kept the mills running day and night by working in **shifts**.

The factory system transformed the textile industry but did not take the place of workshops in all other manufacturing industries. In 1851 only 6 per cent of Britain's total workforce of 9.7 million people worked in textile factories.

Source A   Spinning at home in about 1750

Source B
British exports of textiles

	1784–6	1804–6	1834–6
	Value in £ (and % of all exports)		
All textiles	5,834,000 (43%)	24,391,000 (59%)	32,715,000 (71%)
Cottons	797,000 (6%)	16,339,000 (40%)	22,398,000 (48%)
Woollens	3,882,000 (29%)	6,800,000 (16%)	7,321,000 (16%)

Source C   A cotton mill, 1835

Key words

Linen   Cloth made from flax (a plant grown in Britain and Ireland).
Shifts   Hours taken in turns by teams of workers.

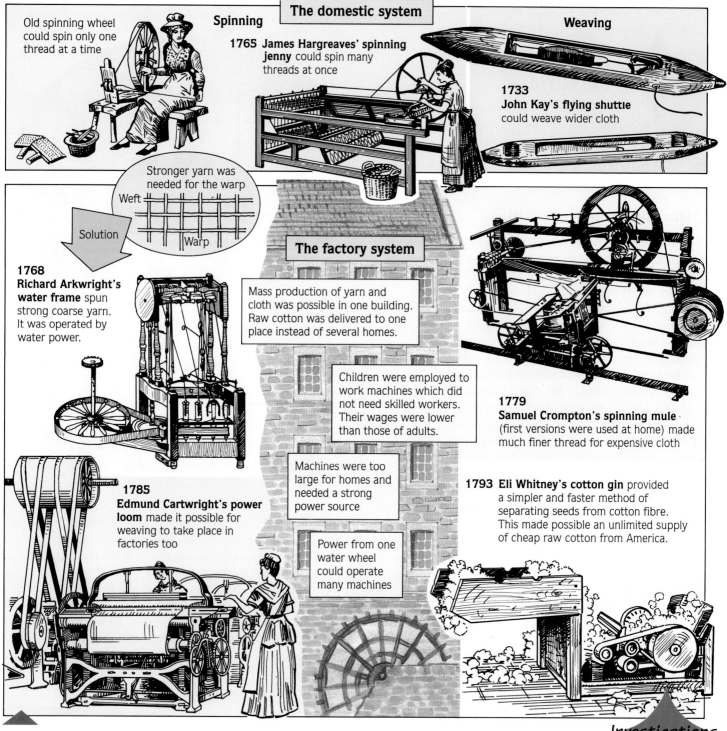

Source D How the factory system began

The following labels appear within the illustration:

The domestic system

Spinning

Old spinning wheel could spin only one thread at a time

1765 James Hargreaves' spinning jenny could spin many threads at once

Weaving

1733 John Kay's flying shuttle could weave wider cloth

Stronger yarn was needed for the warp

Weft / Warp

Solution

1768 Richard Arkwright's water frame spun strong coarse yarn. It was operated by water power.

The factory system

Mass production of yarn and cloth was possible in one building. Raw cotton was delivered to one place instead of several homes.

Children were employed to work machines which did not need skilled workers. Their wages were lower than those of adults.

Machines were too large for homes and needed a strong power source

Power from one water wheel could operate many machines

1785 Edmund Cartwright's power loom made it possible for weaving to take place in factories too

1779 Samuel Crompton's spinning mule (first versions were used at home) made much finer thread for expensive cloth

1793 Eli Whitney's cotton gin provided a simpler and faster method of separating seeds from cotton fibre. This made possible an unlimited supply of cheap raw cotton from America.

The supply of good soft water from the Pennines, the humid climate and the position of Liverpool as a west coast seaport made Lancashire an ideal location for the cotton industry.

Remember...

- **Factories transformed cotton textiles into Britain's most valuable industry.**

Investigations

1 Use Source **B** (page 41) to make three pie charts.
   a) Convert the percentage figures into degrees by multiplying each by 3.6. The new figures should add up to a total of 360.
   b) Use a protractor to measure and draw the angles. Use a different colour for each segment.

2 Use the information and sources to make a spider diagram to explain the expansion of the cotton industry. Here is one already started.

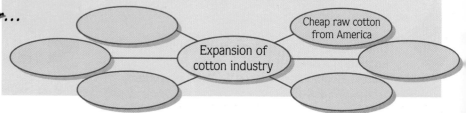

Cheap raw cotton from America

Expansion of cotton industry

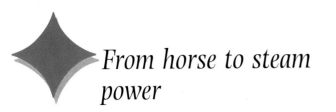

From horse to steam power

Where did the energy come from?

Steam power

Where did the energy come from to grind corn, smelt iron and turn the wheels of factories and new methods of transport?

Steam power was an important breakthrough: steam-powered pumps solved problems of flooding and ventilation in deep coal mines. James Watt's creation of a rotary steam engine in 1781 provided an alternative to the windmill, horse power and water wheel. It made possible a fast new method of land transport, the steam locomotive, and an alternative to sail and muscle power on canals and at sea.

Steam power and the coal and iron industries developed together.

Source A Sources of energy

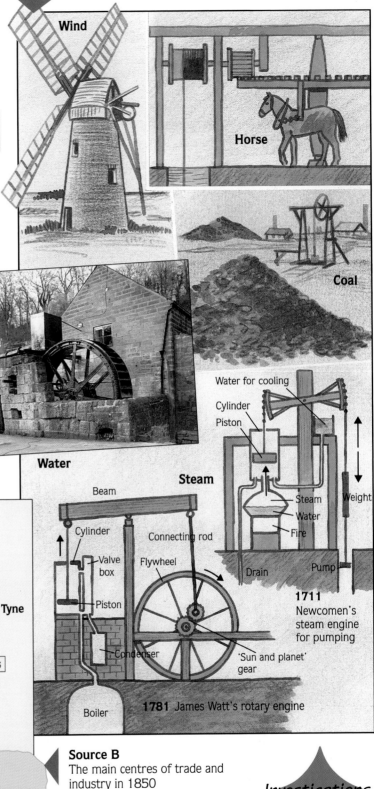

Wind

Horse

Coal

Water for cooling
Cylinder
Piston

Steam
Water
Fire

Weight

Drain

Pump

1711 Newcomen's steam engine for pumping

Water

Steam

Beam

Cylinder

Valve box

Piston

Connecting rod

Flywheel

Condenser

'Sun and planet' gear

Boiler

1781 James Watt's rotary engine

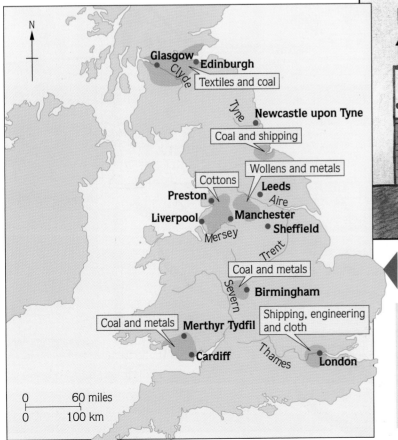

Glasgow
Edinburgh
Clyde
Textiles and coal

Tyne
Newcastle upon Tyne
Coal and shipping

Wollens and metals
Cottons
Leeds
Aire
Preston
Liverpool
Manchester
Sheffield
Mersey
Trent

Coal and metals
Severn
Birmingham

Coal and metals
Merthyr Tydfil
Shipping, engineering and cloth

Cardiff
Thames
London

N

0   60 miles
0   100 km

Source B
The main centres of trade and industry in 1850

Investigations

Look at Source **B**.
a) What parts of Britain became the centres of industry in 1850?
b) Which sources of energy in Source **A** help to explain why these areas developed as centres of industry?

Coal

How did a coal-mine work?

The use of better ways of making iron and the success of steam power greatly increased demand for coal. Coal is a fossil fuel formed over millions of years from vegetation and whole forests crushed between layers of earth and rock. It lies in bands called seams which sometimes break through to the earth's surface.

Methods of mining coal

The easiest way to find coal was to pick it from the surface (open cast mining), dig into the side of hills (drift mining) or dig shallow pits (called bell pits).

Source A Open cast mining, drift mining and a bell pit

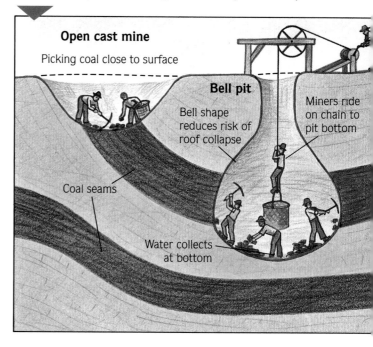

Open cast mine
Picking coal close to surface

Bell pit
Bell shape reduces risk of roof collapse
Miners ride on chain to pit bottom
Coal seams
Water collects at bottom

As surface coal got used up so tunnels got longer and mines got deeper. Mining coal became more difficult and dangerous.

Source B Deep mining

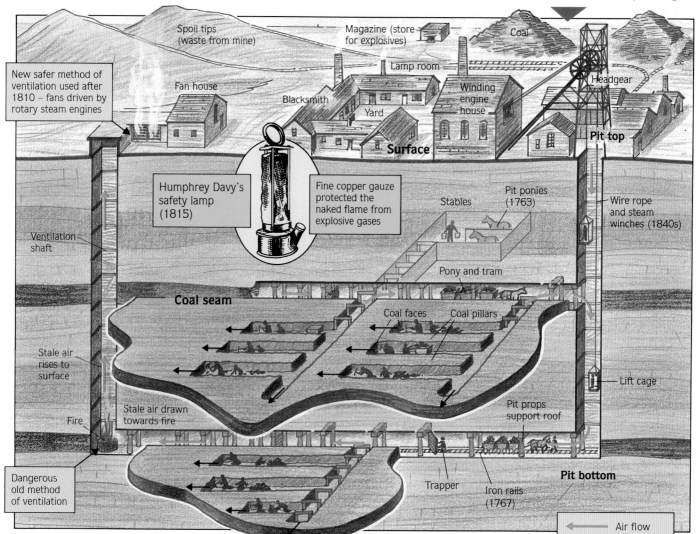

New safer method of ventilation used after 1810 – fans driven by rotary steam engines

Spoil tips (waste from mine)
Magazine (store for explosives)
Coal
Lamp room
Fan house
Blacksmith
Winding engine house
Yard
Headgear
Surface
Pit top

Humphrey Davy's safety lamp (1815)
Fine copper gauze protected the naked flame from explosive gases

Stables
Pit ponies (1763)
Wire rope and steam winches (1840s)

Ventilation shaft

Pony and tram

Coal seam
Coal faces
Coal pillars

Lift cage

Stale air rises to surface

Stale air drawn towards fire

Fire

Pit props support roof

Dangerous old method of ventilation

Trapper
Iron rails (1767)
Pit bottom

← Air flow

44

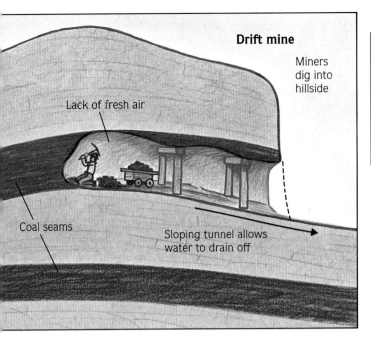

Drift mine

Miners dig into hillside

Lack of fresh air

Coal seams

Sloping tunnel allows water to drain off

Source C Inside a coal-mine near Bilston in Staffordshire

Who did the work?

At the coal face men cut coal in working areas called stalls. Between the stalls they left solid pillars of coal to help support the roof. First they holed or undercut the coal along the floor. This loosened the coal which could then be brought down with a pick. Boys and girls loaded the coal into baskets or onto small trucks called trams which they took away to be lifted to the surface.

A typical job for young children was to work as a trapper opening and shutting the air doors to ensure that fresh air circulated around the mine.

Source D A trapper's description of working in a mine

I have to trap without a light and I am scared. I go at four and sometimes half-past three in the morning and come out at five or half-past. I never go to sleep. Sometimes I sing when I have a light, but not in the dark. I started when I was four years old. When I first went down I couldn't keep my eyes open. I don't fall asleep now; I smokes my pipe.

1842 Report of the Children's Employment Commission

Women and children also looked after the pit ponies and helped blacksmiths who worked in the stables below ground. The ponies lived there and spent all their working lives below ground.

Dangers and some solutions

Miners faced many dangers:
- Roof collapse – wooden posts (pit props) and beams were spaced along tunnels to support the roof.
- Flooding – in 1708 Thomas Newcomen invented a steam-powered pump.
- Gases – poisonous gases, like choke damp, suffocated miners while gases like methane were highly explosive. Miners took caged canaries or small birds into the mine to test out the air. They even tried to explode the gas. John Buddle's steam-powered fan, invented in 1810, replaced the dangerous method of ventilation by lighting fires at the pit bottom (Source **B**). Five years later Sir Humphrey Davy invented a safety lamp which further reduced the risk of explosions.
- Accidents – miners banged their heads and backs on the wooden roof beams, fell, got knocked down by the trams and hit or buried in rock falls.
- Lung disease – 'miner's lung' or pneumoconiosis was caused by inhaling coal dust.

Investigations

Study Sources **A**, **B**, **C** and **D**.

1 List the different kinds of jobs done above and below ground.

2 Why did mines become more dangerous as they got deeper?

3 Why do you think the trapper (Source **D**) was not allowed a light?

4 What inventions helped to make mines safer to work in?

5 For what dangers were there no solutions?

Roads

How were better roads paid for?

In the first part of the eighteenth century there were few good roads. However, farmers, factory and mine owners needed good roads for transporting their goods and for travelling on business. So where did the money to build new roads and repair old ones come from?

Look at Source **A**. Notice the gate across the bridge. This is a clue.

Source A The Devonshire Mail Coach, 1840

BELPER ROAD

Tolls to be let

Notice is hereby Given that a Meeting of the **Trustees** appointed in and by virtue of Acts of Parliament...for repairing, widening, altering and improving the Road from Heage, in the County of Derby, through Belper to Duffield...will be held at the House of George Henn...in Duffield...on Monday, in the Thirteenth day of October next, at Two o'clock in the Afternoon:...the Tolls arriving at the several Toll Gates and Chain upon the said **Turnpike** Road, called or known by the several Names of the Laund Side Gate, Crich road Chain, and Millford Bridge Gate and Side gate, will be offered to be

Let by Auction

To the best Bidder, for the term of one year commencing at twelve Noon of the Eighth day of November next...which tolls are let this present year for the clear Sum of Five Hundred and Twelve Pounds...,and will be put up at that Sum.

Robert Evans
Clerk to the Trustees

Source B

Improved roads made it possible by 1784 for Royal Mail coaches like the one in Source **A** to carry passengers and mail from Bath to London. By 1820 all main towns were linked by coaches like these.

Remember...

- **Roads improved because businessmen formed companies called turnpike trusts to provide the money.**

Investigations

1 What is the purpose of the gate across the bridge in Source **A**?

2 Why did one turnpike road have several toll gates (Source **B**)?

3 Why do you think Acts of Parliament (see Source **B**) were necessary before turnpike roads could be built?

4 Suggest why the trustees sold the right to collect tolls to the highest bidders instead of collecting the tolls themselves (Source **B**).

Key words

Toll Money charged for using a road or bridge.
Trustee Someone who looks after a company's money and how it is spent.
Turnpike A guarded entrance or gateway to a road, where a toll is paid.

Canals

Where were canals built?

Look at the map of inland waterways in 1830 (Source **A**). Notice how the rivers have been linked by waterways and that new waterways or canals have been dug where rivers did not exist.

The Duke of Bridgewater had a canal built in 1759 to carry coal from inside his coal-mine at Worsley to Manchester, 10 miles away. Though he was not the first businessman to build a canal the idea soon became popular.

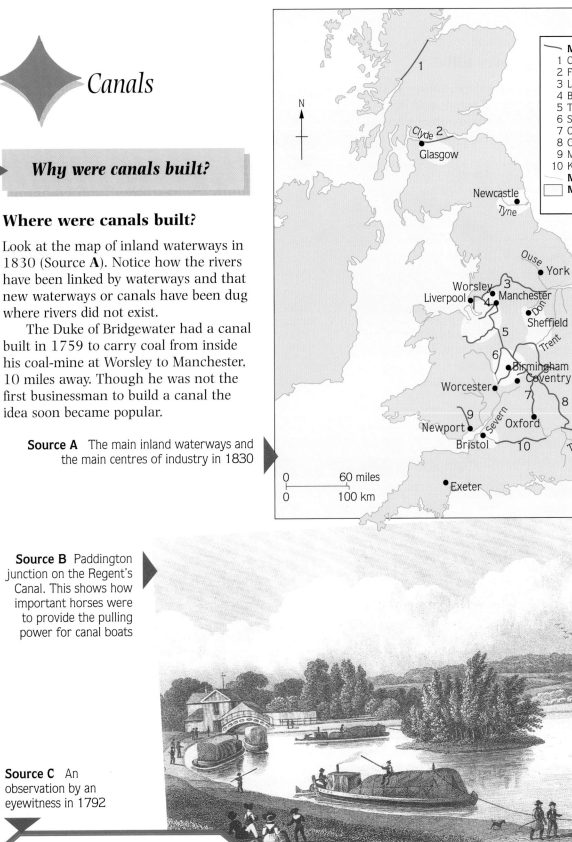

Main canals
1 Caledonian
2 Forth and Clyde
3 Leeds and Liverpool
4 Bridgewater
5 Trent and Mersey (Grand Trunk)
6 Staffordshire and Worcestershire
7 Oxford
8 Grand Junction
9 Monmouth
10 Kennet and Avon
Main rivers
Main industrial areas

Source A The main inland waterways and the main centres of industry in 1830

Source B Paddington junction on the Regent's Canal. This shows how important horses were to provide the pulling power for canal boats

Source C An observation by an eyewitness in 1792

> One horse will draw as much as thirty horses do on the ordinary turnpike roads.
>
> John Phillips, *General History of Inland Navigation*, 1792

Waterways became a more important system of transport than roads because they reduced the cost of carrying goods by half. The busiest time of canal building was between 1790 and 1830.

How did canals go over hills?

Unlike roads, canals cannot slope. Source **D** shows how engineers who designed canals and the **navvies** who built them overcame the technical problems.

Source D Aqueducts, tunnels, cuttings and locks

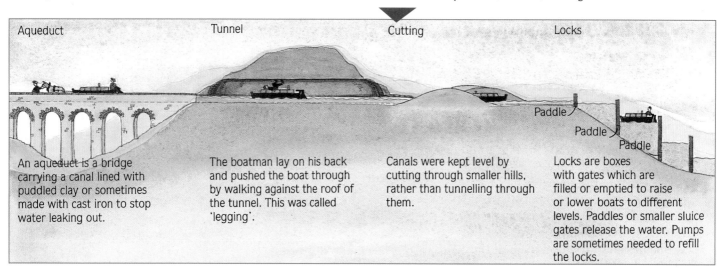

Aqueduct

An aqueduct is a bridge carrying a canal lined with puddled clay or sometimes made with cast iron to stop water leaking out.

Tunnel

The boatman lay on his back and pushed the boat through by walking against the roof of the tunnel. This was called 'legging'.

Cutting

Canals were kept level by cutting through smaller hills, rather than tunnelling through them.

Locks

Locks are boxes with gates which are filled or emptied to raise or lower boats to different levels. Paddles or smaller sluice gates release the water. Pumps are sometimes needed to refill the locks.

Paddle
Paddle
Paddle

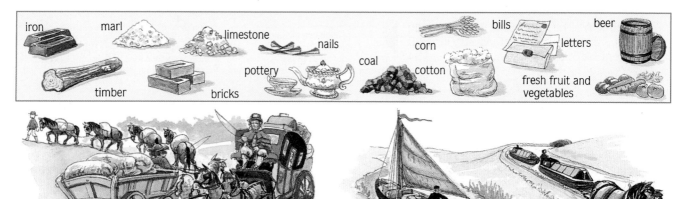

iron marl limestone nails corn bills beer letters coal cotton pottery timber bricks fresh fruit and vegetables

- Canals halved the cost of carrying heavy, bulky and fragile goods.

- Canals solved the problem of carrying essential supplies to industry such as coal for fuel.

- Huge supplies of raw cotton could reach inland cotton mills from ports like Liverpool.

- Farmers could get lime and marl more easily to improve the soil.

- Large quantities of food could travel cheaply to cities like London, Manchester and Liverpool.

Remember...

Source E Better by road or by water?

Investigations

1 Look at Source **D**.
   a) Find four solutions to the problem of keeping canals level.
   b) What difficulties and dangers would the navvies who built these solutions have experienced?

2 Imagine you had to give advice about the best way to transport goods in 1790. The choice is between water and road transport.

   Look at Source **E** and say which of the goods you would send by road and which by water. Give at least two reasons for your decisions.

3 Suggest one disadvantage of using canals.

Key words

Navvies Short for 'inland navigators'; a name for labourers who build roads, canals and railways.

Railways

Who built the railways?

Engineers

An event in 1825 demonstrated that canals would soon lose their place as the best system of **freight** transport. On a railway line built to carry coal from Stockton to Darlington a new kind of steam engine was used. The engine was mounted on a railway carriage and was powerful enough to turn the wheels and pull other carriages behind it. It was a locomotive. The engineer who built the Stockton to Darlington line was George Stephenson. In 1829 he won a competition for the best design for a steam locomotive, which was called the 'Rocket'. This worked on the Manchester to Liverpool railway line which opened in 1830.

Within ten years railways became the most popular form of goods and passenger transport. Soon a network of railway lines criss-crossed the country (Source **A**) often running parallel to canals and stealing their customers.

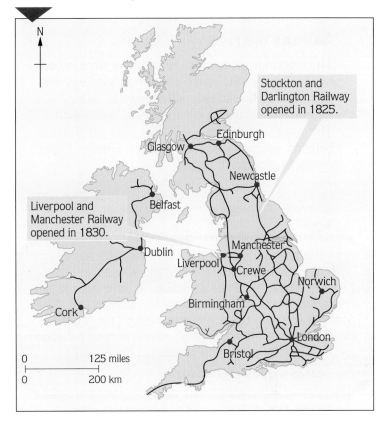

Source A   The railway network in 1852

The engineers like George Stephenson and Isambard Kingdom Brunel who built railways faced similar problems to the canal engineers (Source **B**).

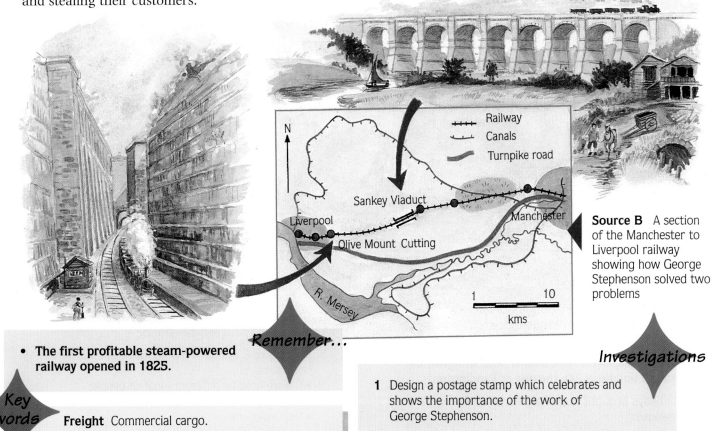

Source B   A section of the Manchester to Liverpool railway showing how George Stephenson solved two problems

Remember...

• **The first profitable steam-powered railway opened in 1825.**

Investigations

1   Design a postage stamp which celebrates and shows the importance of the work of George Stephenson.

Key words

Freight Commercial cargo.

Railway navvies

The labourers who built the railways were called by the same name as the canal builders: navvies. They had to be exceptionally tough to work without modern digging and lifting equipment. The work was dangerous. There were no sickness benefits, pensions, or laws to make employers pay compensation for injuries.

Source D A newspaper report of the death of a navvy

W e are pained to state that a labourer, who was working in the excavation of the rail-road, at Edgehill, where the tunnel is intended to come out and join the surface of the ground, was killed on Monday last. The poor fellow was in the act of undermining a heavy head of clay, fourteen or fifteen feet high, when the mass fell upon him, and literally crushed his bowels out of his body.

Liverpool Mercury, **10 August 1827**

What difference did railways make?

Railways were not new but steam locomotives were one of the most important causes of the transformation of Britain. Look at the scene at the railway station in 1862 (Source **E**).

Source E Paddington Station, London, painted by W.P. Frith in 1862

Investigations

Remember...

- **Thousands of tough labourers called navvies did the hard, dangerous work of building the railways.**

- **Railway engineers, like Brunel, also designed the station buildings like the one at Paddington.**

- **Railways brought about big social and economic changes.**

1 Describe the appearance of the navvies in Source **C**.

2 How does Source **D** show that the work done by navvies was hard and dangerous?

3 Use Source **E** to find and describe clues to show how railways:
   - were used by different kinds of people;
   - increased the demand for coal and iron;
   - created jobs.

Steamships

Did steamships make Britain stronger?

Steamships driven by paddle wheels began to appear from 1804. By 1818 there were regular short distance steam services from Britain to Ireland and France, from Liverpool to Glasgow and on rivers such as the Clyde. By 1825 ships using a mixture of sail and steam had crossed the Atlantic to America and reached India via the Cape of Good Hope. Soon packet steamers provided a reliable world mail service.

Steamships grew in importance at the same time as the sudden expansion of Britain's Empire in the second half of the nineteenth century. Where there were navigable rivers and lakes steamships carried explorers and missionaries like David Livingstone into the interior of continents and opened up new routes for trade (Source **B**). They could bring armed protection and reinforcements when necessary. However, it was not until important technical improvements (Source **C**) that steamships became serious rivals to sailing ships over long distances. The opening of the Suez Canal in 1869, which suited steam power rather than sail, greatly shortened the distance to India and the Far East (Sources **A** and **D**). Steamships overtook the number of sailing ships used for long distances by 1890. Within ten years 70 per cent of British ships were steamers and British ships carried over half of the world's cargoes. Shipbuilding became one of Britain's four most important industries and sources of employment.

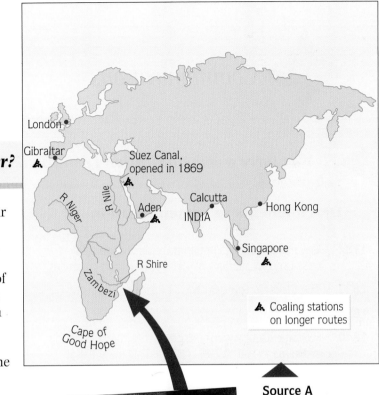

Source A
Steamships needed coaling stations

Source B
David Livingstone's paddle-steamer on the River Shire in 1858

Iron and steel made bigger, lighter ships with thinner sides than wood. This allowed more space for fuel and cargo.

1838	Screw propeller proved better than paddles.
1848	Tubular boiler gave high pressure steam.
1854	Compound engine.
1870s	Quadruple expansion engine.
1884	Turbine engine.

Source C
Technical improvements

Source D   Distance saved by the Suez Canal compared with the route via The Cape of Good Hope

London to Calcutta	32%
London to Singapore	29%
London to Hong Kong	26%

Remember...

- **Steamships helped open up new opportunities for trade and influence where there were navigable rivers and lakes.**

- **The availability of iron and coal and the development of steamships helped Britain become the world's leading shipbuilder and carrier of cargoes.**

Investigations

1 What different uses might David Livingstone have made of his ship (Source **B**)?

2 How can you tell that it is probably an old steamship? (Look at Source **C**.)

3 Why might this picture give a false impression of the importance of steamships to Britain at this time?

Communications

Was there a communication revolution?

Developments in communication

1784	Royal Mail coaches began to replace mounted post-boys as carriers of letters over long distances.
1837	The **electric telegraph** was first used by railways.
1838	Railways began to carry mail.
1840	Postage stamps were introduced at the suggestion of Rowland Hill (1795–1879). This meant that letters were prepaid by the sender rather than paid on delivery by the receiver.
1851	The first underwater cable carrying a telegraph wire linked Dover to Calais.
1866	A transatlantic cable was laid.

1876	Alexander Graham Bell invented the telephone. Private companies use telephones from the 1880s.
1884	Gotfried Daimler rode the first motorcycle powered by a petrol engine.
1885	Carl Benz drove the first car powered by a petrol engine. The first trams were powered by electricity. The 'safety' bicycle was invented.
1896	Guglielmo Marconi founded a company to make equipment capable of sending **wireless** messages in **Morse code** overseas. It was first used in ships.
1900	The whole world was linked by telegraph cable.

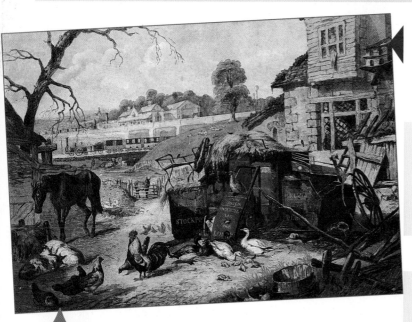

Source B 'Past and Present' engraved by the Leighton brothers. This is a comment on the effect of the coming of railways on road transport

Remember...

Between 1784 and 1900, in addition to faster methods of transport and delivering letters, three new ways of communicating over a distance developed:

* telegraph   * telephone   * wireless.

Investigations

1 Look at Source **B**.
 a) Describe which parts of the picture represent the past and which parts represent the present.
 b) Suggest which other developments in communication described above help to explain the wreckage in the yard shown in Source **B**.

2 With a partner
 a) brainstorm the ways in which developments in communications between 1750 and 1900 would have changed people's lives.
 b) design an advertisement for the first car powered by a petrol engine.

Key words

Electric telegraph A system of communicating over a distance by electrical impulses sent along a wire.
Morse code A system of communicating in short and long impulses or sounds, with written dots and short lines.
Wireless A method of communicating over a distance without wires using electromagnetic waves.

Depth Study: Arkwright and Brunel

Arkwright's story

Richard Arkwright was born in Preston in 1732, the son of a poor labourer and the youngest of 13 children. He tried to make a living as a a barber and wig-maker and, for a short while, ran a public house. His first wife died leaving him to bring up his only son until he remarried – to a woman who may have had enough money to keep him out of prison for debt. They had a daughter but later separated.

It was probably while touring the country buying hair for making wigs that Arkwright discovered that there was a fortune to be made by the person who discovered a faster way of spinning the yarn needed for weaving cloth. In 1768 he developed a large spinning machine which could be powered by a water wheel. Several of these machines in one building, called a mill or a factory, transformed the method of producing yarn for weaving.

Within ten years Arkwright had become very rich and had formed partnerships to build cotton mills in different parts of England and in Scotland. Another invention in 1775, 'the crank and comb' for carding and preparing cotton for spinning made him even richer.

Arkwright's machines put skilled workers out of work causing violent protests. After rioters burned down one of his mills at Birkacre in 1779 he fortified his mill at Cromford with 1500 small arms and a battery of cannon.

He quarrelled with his business partners and made enemies who helped persuade Parliament not to renew the **patents** on his inventions. Nevertheless, Arkwright became High Sheriff of Derbyshire and used his position and wealth to demonstrate his loyalty to King George III who rewarded him with a knighthood.

He suffered from asthma and did not live long enough to move into a splendid new home he had built, called Willersley Castle. When he died in 1792 his personal property was said to be worth about £500 000.

Source A Arkwright's factory at Cromford which worked day and night

Brunel's story

Isambard Kingdom Brunel (1806–59) was the son of a brilliant French engineer, Marc Brunel, who had supported King Louis XVI and escaped from France during the revolution. Isambard received the best possible training as an engineer from his father and a family friend, the famous machine tool-maker, Henry Maudslay.

After several early disappointments Isambard's luck changed when he won a competition in 1830 to build the Clifton Suspension Bridge over the River Avon in Bristol. Source **B** (page 54) shows the range of projects which followed.

Key words

Patent A legal document granted to an inventor giving him the sole right to make, use and sell his invention. It is illegal to copy or make money out of the invention without a licence from the inventor.

1830   Won competition to build Clifton Suspension Bridge over the River Avon in Bristol.

1833   Began improvements to Bristol docks. Appointed engineer to the Great Western Railway.

1838   The transatlantic steamship *Great Western*, launched.

1841   The Great Western Railway completed.

1843   The steamship, *Great Britain*, launched.

1848   Built railway in Devon powered by atmospheric pressure.

1854   Began a bridge at Saltash over the River Tamar.

1855   Built a hospital (assembled from iron parts) for soldiers in the Crimean war.

1858   Launched a huge steamship, the *Great Eastern*, designed to sail around the world without refuelling.

The Great Western Railway was Brunel's most successful project. It involved not only designing railway stations, tunnels and bridges; deciding the width of the track (the gauge) and supervising the details of building the railway but also persuading Parliament to grant permission.

His steamship, *Great Britain*, launched in 1843 was the first ship built entirely of iron and powered by a propeller instead of steam paddles. Despite early disasters, which included running aground, the *SS Great Britain* acted as a troop ship during the Crimean war (1854–6) and Indian Mutiny (1857) and for 23 years sailed regularly to Australia where it carried the first all-England cricket team in 1861.

His last important project, the *Great Eastern*, was a disastrous end to Brunel's career: problems with an untrustworthy business partner, John Scott Russell, worries about finding the money, and overwork ruined Brunel's health and led to a stroke. He died in 1859 shortly after news of an explosion on board the *Great Eastern* during its first sea trials.

What were they like?

White silk cravat.

Long woollen overcoat which would have been tight fitting at the waist and cut away into tails.

It was the fashion for men to have close shaven heads and to wear curled, powdered wigs.

Long silk waistcoat reached below the top of the breeches (trousers cut off at the knee). Men wore long stockings (made of silk, cotton or wool) which folded above the knee and tucked under the ends of the breeches.

Black leather shoes were in fashion with metal buckles.

Source D Isambard Kingdom Brunel (1806–59). What changes in fashion had taken place between the times of Arkwright and Brunel?

Top hat worn straight as was the fashion.

Medium length hair and side-burns.

Pointed standing collar and bow tie.

In 1840s an extra buttonhole (for a flower) in the left lapel became fashionable.

Short waistcoat with lapels.

Morning coats like these were popular in the 1850s.

Trousers and jacket are not a matching suit though both are made of a heavy wool fabric which sags and creases. Note the buttons on the outer seams.

Stacked heels.

High-set slanting pockets.

Watch and chain.

Wide square-toed boots, typical of the 1850s.

Source E The rough draft of a letter written by Arkwright's partner, Jedidiah Strutt, to another partner, John Smalley in 1773

We can not (*stop his mouth or prevent his wrong doing*) prevent his saying ill natured things nor can we regulate his actions...

(The words in italic were crossed out before making a final copy.)

Source F In October 1780 James Watt, the inventor of the rotative steam engine, wrote to his friend, Matthew Boulton

Mr Arkwright sent for me last night, he has built a mill and the miners have let down his water so that it cannot move. He is much more modest than he was the last time but despises your India Reels [for winding silk]. He says he can make a thing for that purpose to answer as well for a shilling a piece...

At Cromford Arkwright built homes for his workers, a hotel and a chapel and provided a festival for them every year.

Source G A doctor, Sylas Neville, who visited Cromford in 1781 was impressed

By his conduct [Arkwright] appears to be a man of great understanding and to know the way of making his people do their best. He not only distributes **pecuniary rewards**, but gives distinguishing dresses to the most deserving of both sexes...He also gives two Balls at the Greyhound to the workmen, and their wives and families with a week's jubilee at the time of each ball. This makes them industrious and sober all the rest of the year.

Key words **Pecuniary rewards** Money.

Source H How a friend remembered Brunel

He could enter into the most boyish pranks and fun, without in the least distracting his attention from the matter of business...
I believe that a more joyous nature, combined with the highest intellectual faculties, was never created...
I believe at that time he scarcely ever went to bed, though I can never remember to have seen him tired or out of spirits. He was a very constant smoker, and would take his nap in an armchair very frequently with a cigar in his mouth...
I have never known a man who, possessing courage which to many would appear almost like rashness, was less disposed to trust to chance or to throw away any chance of attaining his object...

Memoir of St George Burke KC

Source I A letter from Brunel to an assistant

Plain, gentlemanly language seems to have no effect upon you. I must try stronger language and stronger measures. You are a cursed, lazy, inattentive, apathetic vagabond, and if you continue to neglect my instructions, and to show such infernal laziness, I shall send you about your business.

Source J Brunel kept a diary. At the age of 21 he wrote:

After all I shall most likely remain a bachelor and that is I think best for me. My profession is after all my only fit wife...

Journal, 1827

Source K Brunel, writing in his diary eight years later:

I have made my fortune or rather the foundation of it and have taken Lord Devon's house, No. 18 Duke St – a fine house – I have a fine travelling carriage – I go sometimes with my four horses – I have a cab and horse, I have a secretary – in fact I am now somebody. Everything has prospered, everything at this moment is in sunshine. I don't like it – it can't last – bad weather must surely come...I foresee one thing – this time 12 months I shall be a married man. How will that be? Will it make me happier?

Journal, Boxing Night, 1835

How historians have judged Arkwright and Brunel

Source L One historian of the cotton industry doubted if Arkwright was the real inventor of his first spinning machine

His abilities consisted solely in having cunning enough to pump a secret out of a silly, talkative clockmaker and having sense enough to know when he saw a good invention.

Richard Guest, 1823

Source M By the historian Edward Baines

To Arkwright [and Watt] England is far more indebted for her triumphs than to Nelson or Wellington. Without the means supplied by her flourishing manufactures and trade, the country would not have born up under a conflict so prolonged and exhausting [war with France].

E. Bains, *The Cotton Manufacture in Great Britain*, 1835

Source N By one of Brunel's biographers

Between 1760 and 1860 a comparatively small group of men transformed the face of England...of this small group of men...Isambard Brunel was perhaps the outstanding personality.

L.T.C. Rolt, *Isambard Kingdom Brunel*, 1957

Investigations

1 a) Describe your first feelings and thoughts about Arkwright and Brunel after looking at their pictures and studying Sources **E** to **N**.
    b) Which of Sources **C** to **N** do you least trust and why?

2 What reasons can you find in Chapters 4 and 5 to agree or disagree with the historians' judgements of Arkwright and Brunel in Sources **M** and **N**?

3 Imagine it has been decided to rename your school after a famous person to improve its image. The person has to be either Arkwright or Brunel. Design a leaflet to persuade people to make the right choice.

Why did the population grow so fast?

In 1750 about 6.5 million people lived in England, Wales and Scotland; 3 million lived in Ireland. A clergyman and economist, Thomas Malthus (1766–1834) believed that **epidemics**, famine and war were nature's way of keeping a balance between population and food supply. He blamed the increase in the population on methods of looking after the poor where help depended on the size of their families. He believed this encouraged the poor to marry early and have large families.

Historians have argued rather than agreed about why population growth suddenly accelerated from about 1780.

Source A Population changes in the United Kingdom 1751–1901

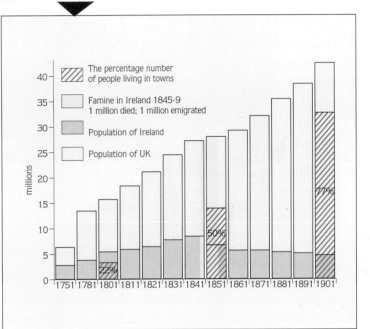

Source B One historian's view of the cause of population growth:

> Such evidence as there is at present would lean much more heavily towards lower **mortality** as an explanation of population growth than towards changes in marriage and fertility.
>
> **D.V. Glass, 1965**

Source C Another historian suggested that because the Industrial Revolution created more jobs it encouraged people to have more children. He asked:

> Did the Industrial Revolution create its own labour force?
>
> **H.J. Habakkuk, 1958**

Source D Eric Evans disagreed:

> The rise in the population of Britain during the eighteenth century...acted as a spur to industrial development in Britain since it provided not only a potential workforce for workshop and factory but also rising demand for industrial goods.
>
> **E.J. Evans, 1983**

Investigations

1 Look at Source **A**.
   a) What evidence is there to support the views of Thomas Malthus on nature's way of controlling population growth?
   b) What changed about where people lived?

2 **a)** Which of Sources **B**, **C** and **D** suggest a different explanation from Malthus for the rapid rise of the population shown in Source **A**? Explain the differences.
   b) If Glass (Source **B**) is correct, suggest possible causes of 'lower mortality'.

3 Does Eric Evans (Source **D**) prove that Habakkuk (Source **C**) was wrong? Explain your answer.

Remember...

- **The population of Britain suddenly accelerated in the second half of the eighteenth century and trebled by 1901. The reason why is still not clear.**

Key words

Epidemic When a disease spreads quickly, affecting many people.
Mortality Number of deaths.

Towns

Source A
Sheffield in about 1850

By 1850 half of the population lived in towns where jobs were easier to find. Towns grew around centres of industry and trade.

As the centres of towns became crowded more new homes were built on the outskirts or suburbs. Those who could afford to moved out to the new homes. Poorer people moved in to occupy the older houses in the town centres. The new homes were built close to good roads or railway lines so that people could travel to work easily. In this way towns expanded and changed in character.

Source B Population of towns

	1801	1851	1871
Glasgow	77,000	345,000	522,000
Newcastle-upon-Tyne	33,000	88,000	128,000
Liverpool	82,000	376,000	493,000
Sheffield	46,000	135,000	240,000
Manchester	75,000	303,000	351,000
Birmingham	71,000	233,000	344,000
London	959,000	2,362,000	3,254,000
Merthyr Tydfil	8,000	46,000	52,000
Bristol	55,000	137,000	183,000

Investigations

1 Look at Source **A**. With a partner see who is the first to find the following:
   - five churches
   - high street
   - canal
   - railway
   - mine
   - millstones
   - blast furnaces and forges
   - woman carrying water on her head
   - woman doing the washing outdoors
   - gas streetlight

2 Look at how the population of Sheffield grew between 1801 and 1851 (Source **B**). What changes to Sheffield would the grandparents of the children in Source **A** have been able to describe?

3 What problems would the growth of these towns have caused for
   a) people's health
   b) keeping law and order?

Remember...

- **By the end of the nineteenth century most British people lived in towns.**

Social classes

Did society become more divided?

Source **A** shows three classes of travel on the Manchester to Liverpool railway. It also shows three social classes of people who used them:

- the very rich whose wealth came from land and property.
- the middle classes who included professions such as doctors, lawyers, bankers, architects, engineers, clergymen, teachers, civil servants, army and naval officers, businessmen and shop owners.
- the working classes who included industrial workers, farm labourers, soldiers, sailors, dockers and servants.

What caused Britain to be divided into social classes?

Like all countries wealth divided people into those who had wealth, those who had some more than others and those who had little or nothing. But it was not just wealth which decided which class people belonged to. It had more to do with the different ways people earned a living and how much power or advantage this gave them over each other. Between 1750 and 1900 people's awareness of social class became more intense as a result of new job opportunities and changes in working and living conditions.

Investigations

Look at Source **A**.
a) Describe the differences between the three classes of travel.
b) Suggest why people are pushing to get on the middle-class carriage.

Source A   Three classes of travel on the Manchester to Liverpool railway

FIRST CLASS.

SECOND CLASS.

THIRD CLASS.

• As the population grew and towns expanded more civil servants were needed to run the government. There was a need for more doctors, lawyers, bankers and other middle-class professions. To get these jobs education and qualifications became more important.

• New factories, workshops and mines brought together large numbers of workers whose similar standard of living and way of life made them feel separate as a class from their employers and professional people.

• The gap between the rich and poor widened causing tensions between the classes. Snobbery and jealousies hardened into attitudes of 'them' and 'us'. Social differences were judged by what people wore, where they lived, the way they spoke and how many servants they had. Even the poorest middle-class family had a maid. Books published on the rules of etiquette (manners) were carefully read for fear of being caught out.

The mixing of the social classes in public places, such as the Great Exhibition of 1851, was a cause for comment (Source **B**). Artists took care to draw attention to visual clues such as clothing (Source **C**).

Source B 'Whoever thought of meeting you here?' A cartoon from *Punch*, 1851, commenting on the mixing of the social classes at the Great Exhibition

Source C *Work* by F.M. Brown, 1852–65. This section of the painting shows navvies working and people passing by on a London street

Investigations

1 Look at Source **B**. The Great Exhibition of 1851 was organised to show off the achievements of Britain's Industrial Revolution. This cartoon is a joke from the magazine, *Punch*, which was read by the rich and middle classes.
  a) How can you tell that the people meeting here come from different social classes?
  b) Explain the joke.

2 Look at Source **C**.
  a) Use these descriptions to find the following:
  • Two middle-class women wearing shallow bonnets worn far back on the head tied with ribbon, shawl-mantles, gloves and day dresses worn over hooped petticoats, known as 'crinoline'.
  • Two navvies wearing stocking caps. One has a loose shirt and long cord trousers hitched up at the knee with 'yarks' (string); the other is wearing a plain smock tucked into old fashioned breeches and thick woollen socks. On their feet are lace-up 'blucher' boots.
  • The foreman with bow tie, linen shirt, fancy waistcoat and watch and chain under his linen apron.
  b) How does the artist use women in this picture to show big differences between the rich and the poor?
  c) How does the artist use the dogs to show differences in social classes?
  d) Why do you think the foreman is dressed differently to the two navvies?
  e) Which classes of people lived in this part of London? How can you tell?

Remember...

• **The Industrial Revolution intensified social differences by strengthening the middle classes and creating a new class of industrial workers.**

Working conditions

How safe were working conditions?

The Industrial Revolution resulted in many cases of horrific working conditions.

Robert Blincoe was an orphan sent from a workhouse in London at the age of seven to work in a cotton mill in the north of England.

Source A From *A memoir of Robert Blincoe, an Orphan boy* by John Brown, 1828

T he [job] first [given] to him was to pick up the loose cotton that fell upon the floor. Apparently nothing could be easier...although [he was] much terrified by the...noise of the machinery.
When his turn to suffer came, the fore-finger of his left hand was caught and almost before he could cry out, off was the first joint...he clapped the [squashed] joint, streaming with blood, and ran off to...the surgeon, who...put the parts together again and sent him back to the mill.

Source B An illustration from *Life and Adventures of Michael Armstrong, Factory Boy*, written in 1840 by Frances Trollope

The safety of working conditions in coal mines may be judged from Source **C**.

Source C Deaths caused by accidents in coal mines in 1838, from a Parliamentary report

Cause of death	Under 13 years of age	13 and not exceeding 18 years of age	Above 18 years of age
Fell down the shafts	13	16	31
Fell down the shaft from the rope breaking	1		2
Fell out when ascending			3
Drawn over the pulley	3		3
Fall of stone out of a skip down the shaft	1		3
Drowned in the mines	3	4	15
Fall of stones, coal and rubbish in the mines	14	14	69
Injuries in coal pits, the nature of which is not specified	6	3	32
Crushed in coal pits		1	1
Explosion of gas	13	18	49
Suffocated by chokedamp [air low in oxygen]		2	6
Explosion of gunpowder		1	3
By tram waggons	4	5	12
Total	58	64	229

Chimney sweeps had to climb inside chimneys to push brushes up the flues. They developed unpleasant forms of skin cancer but these were the least of their worries. Often the chimneys were still hot and there was a risk of getting stuck (Source **E**).

Source D A London chimney sweep

Source E Evidence on the death of a climbing boy, 29 March 1813, given to a Parliamentary committee, 1817

A n alarm was given in the brewhouse immediately that he had stuck in the chimney, and a bricklayer who was at work near the spot attended, and after knocking down part of the brickwork of the chimney, just above the fireplace, made a hole sufficiently large to draw him through...the elbows and knees, seemed burnt to the bone; from which it must be evident that the unhappy sufferer made some attempts to return as soon as the horrors of his situation became apparent.

In the glove-making industry some workers started work very young.

Source F The evidence of Mary Thorpe from Bulwell near Nottingham to a Children's Employment Commission, 1863

C hildren younger than seven are kept up till eleven and twelve. Mothers will pin them to their knee to keep them to their work, and if they are sleepy give them a slap on the head to keep them awake...My little sister, now five, can stitch a good many little fingers, and is very clever, having been at it for two years.

Making matches was just one of many industries which used dangerous chemicals. Matches had to be dipped into a mixture of phosphorus and glue. Working with the fumes caused a frightening disease called phossy jaw. This would start with a cold then toothache (Source **G**).

Source G A description of the disease phossy jaw

A fter a while] the pain is no longer confined to the teeth, but spreads to the whole of the upper and lower jaws...the throat glands swell and become painful, the gum becomes inflamed, and...soft and elastic...abscesses [sores]...form which discharge loathsome and putrid matter...the teeth become loose, and either fall out of themselves, or may be easily pulled out by the fingers...In some cases the whole gum, the bone, the cheek, and even the throat, have been eaten away by the terrible disease.

Andrea Rabagliati, *Great Industries of Great Britain, Health and Disease in Industrial Britain* c.1880

Remember.

- **These sources show mounting evidence of unsafe working conditions and the kinds of pressure being put on the government to take action to protect workers.**

Investigation

1 Use Sources **A–G** to design a poster which would have made people worry about the working conditions caused by the Industrial Revolution.

2 How does the evidence in these Sources show that people were worried already about working conditions?

Public health

Source A A Court for King Cholera, 1840

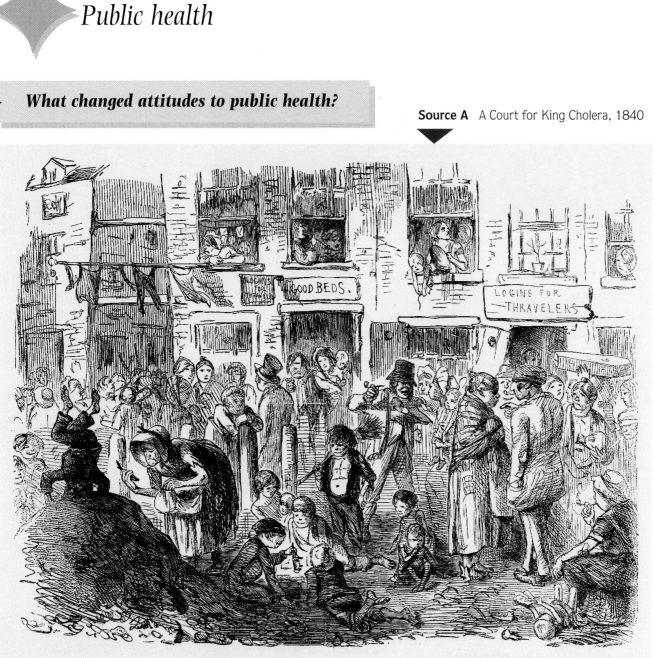

A COURT FOR KING CHOLERA.

During the nineteenth century attitudes to public health care changed dramatically. In 1750 most people were against the idea of the government passing more laws and raising taxes to keep streets clean, build and repair sewers, and ensure a clean water supply. They thought it best to leave people to sort out their own mess rather than pay for it by higher taxes. This attitude, known as ***laissez-faire***, applied to almost all suggestions that the government should interfere to improve people's living and working conditions if it cost the tax payer money. By the 1840s the attitude of *laissez-faire* in public health was being abandoned. People now wanted the government to act and by 1900 there were laws which gave local councils the power to improve street drainage; build sewers, public lavatories, reservoirs, public swimming baths and parks; clear slums and provide better housing.

Key words

Laissez-faire The idea that it was best for governments to interfere with people's lives and the economy as little as possible and so avoid high taxes.

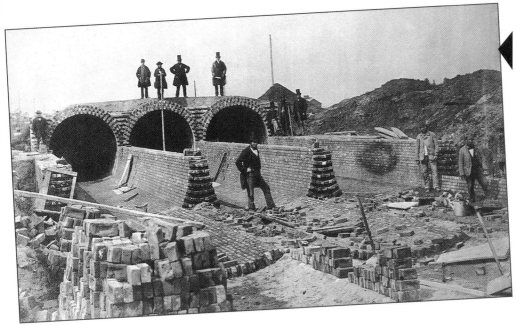

● *Pollution* Industrial pollution polluted the air and environment. Human and industrial waste polluted rivers and the water supplies.

● *Epidemics* Where there was overcrowding and poor **sanitation** infectious diseases like tuberculosis spread easily, as did diseases spread by water like cholera and typhoid. Two serious epidemics of cholera in 1831–2 (21 000 deaths) and in 1849–50 (50 000) frightened people as well as caused misery. In 1861 Queen Victoria's husband, Prince Albert, died of typhoid.

● *Political change* Middle-class people and working people gained more political power and voted for change.

● *The media* Newspapers and magazines took an active interest in public health. The cartoons of *Punch* (Source **A**) are an example of how they tried to influence opinion.

● *Edwin Chadwick (1800–1890)* Chadwick was a determined and tireless civil servant who led a government investigation into the *Sanitary Condition of the Labouring Population*. The interest and discussion that followed his reports led to the first Public Health Act in 1848.

● *Breakthroughs in understanding the cause of disease* A popular theory was that miasma (smells) caused disease. However, in 1854 a London doctor, John Snow, proved that contaminated water caused the spread of cholera. Then, in 1861, Louis Pasteur proved that diseases were caused by tiny creatures (germs or microbes).

Public Health Acts

● 1848 Public Health Act: set up a Central Board of Health in London which could force towns to have a Health Board if the death-rate of a town was 23 in every 1000. The Boards could set a rate (tax) to pay for street cleaning, proper drainage and sewers.

● 1864 Factory Act: made employers provide healthier conditions for workers, such as ventilation.

● 1866 Sanitary Act: sanitary inspectors in every town had powers to order landlords to clean up their houses and stop overcrowding them.

● 1875 Public Health Act: there had to be a Health Inspector and a Sanitary Officer in towns. Every district had to have a Public Health Committee to get rid of rubbish, sewage, slum housing, and to provide clean water, healthy conditions in workplaces, and to inspect food and markets.

● 1876 Acts: building regulations were laid down to improve standards of house building and laws passed against polluting rivers.

Why did attitudes change?

The change of attitudes to public health care had several causes. Is it possible to judge which was the most important?

● *The growth of towns* The population of towns grew faster than new houses and improved water supplies or sewers could be built.

Investigations

1 a) What dangers to health are shown in Source **A**?
b) If the real cause of disease was not known until 1861, how do you explain the clues in this cartoon about the cause of cholera?

2 Look at Source **B**.
a) Why do you think sewers like this were not built in the early 1800s?
b) Why is it not likely that Pasteur's discovery of the real cause of disease explains why these sewers were being built?

3 The list of causes of the change in attitudes to public health are not placed in any order and the list does not show how they link together. Decide on an order which makes sense and draw a diagram or flow chart of key headings to show the links between them.

Key words

Sanitation Practical ways to ensure public health, such as a clean water supply.

Workhouses for the poor

Were changes to the Poor Law in 1834 a success?

Before 1834 each parish church looked after the poor. Those too young, too old or sick were cared for in a poorhouse while the **able-bodied** poor lived in their own homes where they received food or money. All this was paid for by the **ratepayers**. Many parishes followed the example of Speenhamland in Berkshire where, from 1795, they used the cost of bread and the size of families to decide how much to give the poor.

Between 1775 to 1832 the cost of looking after the poor soared from £1.5 million to £7 million a year. People disagreed about the causes: some blamed the old poor laws for encouraging idleness and large families; others blamed changes in farming and industry, poor harvests, high food prices, trade depressions and unemployment. A Royal Commission was set up to find a better and less expensive way of dealing with poverty.

Source A   The recommendation of the Royal Commission

First, that except as to medical attendance…all relief whatever to able-bodied persons or to their families, otherwise than in well-regulated workhouses…shall be declared unlawful, and shall cease.

Source B   The workhouse system which began in 1834 meant:

making the workhouse an uninviting place of **wholesome restraint**…

Report of the Royal Commission into the Poor Law, 1834

Source C   Andover workhouse in Hampshire, 1846. This is typical of the design of a new kind of workhouse built to serve a group of parishes

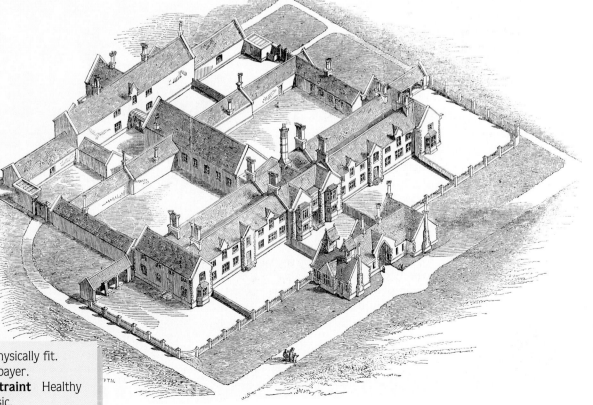

Investigations

What evidence is there in Sources **A**, **B** and **C** that the purpose of the changes to the Poor Law was to discourage the poor from seeking help?

Key words

Able-bodied   Physically fit.
Ratepayer   Taxpayer.
Wholesome restraint   Healthy but strict and basic.

The poor entered a workhouse only after a humiliating interview, called the workhouse test, to prove they deserved to be helped. Families were split up. They had to dress in workhouse clothes and have their hair cut short to reduce the problem of lice. In some workhouses unmarried mothers were made to wear yellow dresses to 'show them up'. Inside the workhouses the windows were too high for people to easily look out and the window ledges sloped to prevent **paupers** putting objects on them. There were no lockers as personal possessions were not allowed.

The routine of the workhouse was as boring as possible. Paupers got up early, assembled for a roll call and prayers, ate meals in silence and then started work. Men did hated jobs like crushing bones for making glue and fertiliser, or picking oakum (untwisting lengths of rope so that the fibres could be reused). Women scrubbed, cleaned, did the washing and prepared the food. Children had at least three hours schooling in reading, writing and the Bible. The diet was healthy but without much variety. Paupers often went hungry.

Source D A description of mealtime in a workhouse in *Oliver Twist*, a novel by Charles Dickens written in 1838

l
ots were cast who should walk up to the master after supper that evening and ask for more; and it fell to Oliver Twist…
'Please, Sir, I want some more…'
The master was a fat healthy man;…He gazed in astonishment on the small rebel… and then clung for support to the copper [large pan]. The assistants were paralysed with wonder; the boys with fear…

Punishments for misbehaviour included missing meals, solitary confinement and beatings.

From most ratepayers' point of view the workhouse system was a terrific success. The cost of looking after the poor was 49 per cent less in 1837 than in 1818. However, high unemployment in northern towns like Preston and Stockport in 1842 caused people to riot rather than enter workhouses (Source **E**). This forced the authorities to continue to give outdoor relief, that is they helped the poor without making them enter workhouses. Nevertheless, by 1900 2.5 per cent of a much larger population received **poor relief** compared with 5.7 per cent of the population in 1850.

Source E The Stockport riots in 1842

Remember…

- **Changes to the Poor Law in 1834 reduced the cost of looking after the poor but did not reduce poverty.**

Key words

Pauper Poor person.
Poor relief Help given to the poor.

Investigations

1 What does Source **D** suggest about the author, Charles Dickens', attitude to the new workhouse system?

2 Why do you think people in northern towns rioted rather than enter workhouses (Source **E**)?

3 Does the fact that the workhouse system lasted until 1948 mean it was a good system for dealing with the poor? Explain your answer.

Crime and punishment

Did the punishment fit the crime?

Over 200 crimes in 1750 carried the death sentence. They included picking pockets (even stealing a handkerchief), slitting a man's nose, cutting down trees, sending threatening letters and poaching.

The treatment of young criminals was the same as for adults (Source **A**).

Until 1868 people were hanged in public and large crowds turned up to watch. In practice juries often refused to convict people for the less serious crimes to prevent them hanging. By about 1830 many of these offences were no longer **capital crimes**. More people went to prison instead.

Prisons

Prisons were overcrowded and filthy. Gaol fever (typhus) spread easily and killed about a quarter of all prisoners each year. One magistrate who wanted to improve conditions in prisons, John Howard, published a shocking report in 1777 on prisons he had visited (Source **B**).

A solution to overcrowded prisons was to transport convicts to the American colonies to work as slave labour but America's War of Independence in 1776 put a temporary stop to this. The shortage of prison space forced the government to convert old ships into floating prisons known as hulks (Source **C**).

Source A A prison reformer from Bristol, J.S. Harford, describes a typical case in 1815

> I saw the irons put upon a little boy ten years old, who had just been brought in for stealing a pound and a half of sugar. He was then introduced into the **felons'** court, crowded with wretches among the most abandoned of their class.

Source B From *State of the Prisons* (1777) by John Howard

> Air which has been breathed is made poisonous to a more intense degree, by the effluvia [vomit] from the sick, and what else in prisons is offensive...my clothes were so offensive that in a post-chaise [carriage] I could not bear the windows drawn up; and was therefore obliged to travel commonly on horseback.

Source C Prison hulks in Portsmouth harbour

Key words

Capital crime A crime carrying the death sentence.
Felon A person who has done a serious crime.

Then in 1787 transportation to Australia began and lasted until 1868. None of the first convicts (548 males and 188 females) shipped to Australia were convicted of serious crimes such as murder or rape. The oldest female, Dorothy Hanland, was 82 and sentenced to 7 years transportation for **perjury**.

Until the government took full responsibility for prisons in 1877 nearly half of Britain's prisons were privately owned and profit making.

Many people, including the parents of both Isambard Brunel and Charles Dickens, spent some time in prison for debt. Debtors and prisoners waiting for trial had to pay for their food and pay a fee to the gaolers before they were released. They depended on money from charity, relatives or friends. Meanwhile they had to mix with convicted criminals of all kinds and ages. Only the sexes were separated. Until 1817 even prisoners waiting for trial were kept in irons.

Prison reform

Reformers like John Howard and Elizabeth Fry drew attention to the appalling conditions inside prisons and campaigned to make them cleaner and to provide activities to improve the minds of prisoners.

From 1820 flogging of women stopped and in 1823 it became illegal for gaolers to make money by selling food, drink and privileges. Female prisoners had female wardens. Prisons began to receive regular visits from chaplains and doctors, and from 1835 there were prison inspectors. Prisons became cleaner. To improve hygiene prisoners had to wear prison uniform and have their hair cut short.

Source D A prisoner's description of a bath

> The first time I saw my bath I was thoroughly disgusted, as the water was not unlike mutton broth [soup].
>
> *Revelations of Prison Life* by *One-who-has-suffered*, 1882

Punishments

From 1816 many prisons had a treadmill. This was a huge wheel with steps turned by the tread of prisoners like 'an ever lasting staircase' (Source **E**). Another unpleasant exercise was the crank which turned a wheel inside a box which scooped and emptied cups of sand. A meter showed if a prisoner had turned the handle enough times to earn his meal of the day. Both treadmill and crank were used until 1898.

Prisons also experimented with separating prisoners (Source **E**) and insisting on silence at all times to prevent prisoners having a bad influence on each other. These prisons had a high number of suicides and prisoners who became mentally ill.

Source E Oakum picking, the separate system and the treadmill (behind the stalls) at Holloway prison

Investigations

Remember...

- **Harsh punishments failed to prevent an increase in crime or in the number of people sent to prison.**

1 If you had been home secretary before 1830, which punishments would you have asked Parliament to end and why?

2 How do you imagine conditions inside prison hulks (Source **C**) compared with conditions in prisons on dry land?

3 How does your idea of what a prison should be like compare with Holloway prison (Source **E**)?

Key words   **Perjury** To lie in court after promising to tell the truth.

Leisure

What did people do for fun?

Compared with the rich (Source **A**) working-class people had little time for leisure. In addition to Sundays, Christmas Day and Good Friday the Factory Act of 1833 gave people under the age of 18 8½ days of unpaid holiday. From 1871 the closure of banks on Easter Monday, the first Monday in August and Boxing Day stopped business and resulted in bank holidays.

The nearest thing poor people living in cities like London had to seasonal holidays were working holidays in the countryside.

Source A The seasons of leisure for the very rich

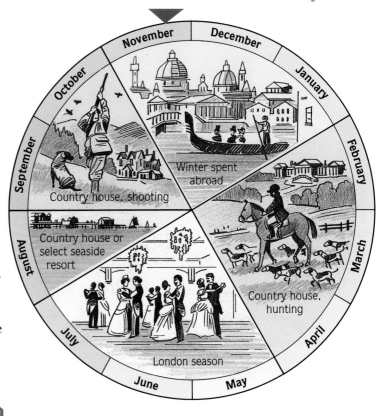

Source B

E very year, in the second week of September, many people went hop-picking. Mostly they were women and children; men only went if they happened to be out of work at the time…It was a working holiday but it meant a change of surroundings, fresh air and freedom to enjoy the evenings when the day's work was finished.

Grace Foakes, *Between High Walls*, **1974**

Did working men have more time for leisure than women? The evidence for this is confusing.

Source C Mrs Shaw, a London health visitor in the 1880s, said that:

W hen the man came home he had his freedom to go out if he wanted to; most of them did nothing in the house, wouldn't even wash up. But the women, they never stopped, and they never had an outing further than the back yard.

G o into any…public house at the corner of the ordinary East End Street – there, standing at the counter or seated on the benches against the wall or partition will be perhaps a dozen people, men and women, chatting together over their beer…

Charles Booth, *Life and Labour of the People of London*, **Macmillan 1902–3**

Betting sports were very popular. From 1824 a law banned cruel sports using animals, like cockfighting and bear-baiting. However, Source **E** shows men of all classes in a pub in about 1850 laying bets on rat-catching.

Source E Rat-catching at the Blue Anchor Tavern, 1850–2

Source D Charles Booth described a different scene

Sports developed more quickly for men than women. Attitudes restricted women. A sun-tan was thought to be 'common' so 'respectable' women covered as much of their skin as possible.

Overarm bowling in cricket was first allowed in 1864 so that women could bowl without their dresses getting in the way.

Source F The development of sport

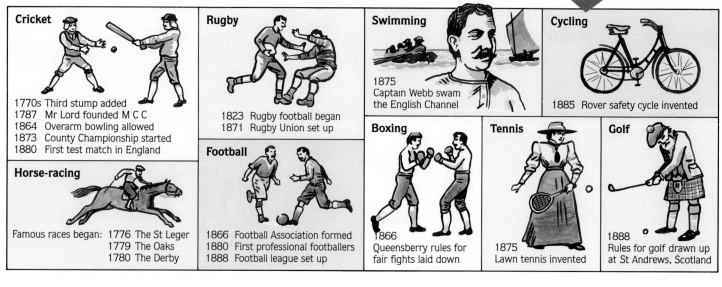

Cricket
1770s Third stump added
1787 Mr Lord founded M C C
1864 Overarm bowling allowed
1873 County Championship started
1880 First test match in England

Horse-racing
Famous races began: 1776 The St Leger
1779 The Oaks
1780 The Derby

Rugby
1823 Rugby football began
1871 Rugby Union set up

Football
1866 Football Association formed
1880 First professional footballers
1888 Football league set up

Swimming
1875 Captain Webb swam the English Channel

Boxing
1866 Queensberry rules for fair fights laid down

Cycling
1885 Rover safety cycle invented

Tennis
1875 Lawn tennis invented

Golf
1888 Rules for golf drawn up at St Andrews, Scotland

Source G When lawn tennis became popular a book on good manners advised women what to wear

> Wool should in some measure form the material, for health's sake, as a preventive of chills being taken… The bodice is usually made full, and the skirt is short [ankle-length] and not burdened with many frills and flounces…hats of every variety are worn.
>
> ***Etiquette of Good Society**, 1893*

Source H A woman's magazine thought it wrong for women to enjoy bicycling

> The mere act of riding a bicycle is not in itself sinful and if it is the only way of reaching the Church on Sunday it may be excusable. On the other hand, if walking or riding in the usual way is discarded for the sake of the exercise or exhilaration bicycle riding affords, it is clearly wrong.
>
> ***Home Companion**, 1885*

For most ordinary people cheap day trips by railway to the seaside or countryside, and visits to fairs, circuses and music halls were popular. At home, without radio or television, families made their own entertainment. Music sheets were cheap (Source **I**) and many homes had a piano.

Source I
A cover of a music sheet by Alfred Concanen, 1886

MARTHA, THE MILKMANS' DAUGHTER.

Remember...

- **Opportunities for leisure were not equal.**

Investigations

1 Look at Sources **A**, **B** and **D** on page 69 and Source **I**. How did leisure for the very rich compare with that of working-class people?

2 Explain which details of Source **C** are supported by the evidence in Source **E**.

3 In what way does the evidence of Source **D** suggest that Source **C** is untrue?

4 Look at Sources **F**, **G**, and **H**. Explain which of the following you think had the least opportunity to enjoy sport and why:
   a) women
   b) working-class men
   c) the rich and middle classes.

Depth Study: History around us

Novels

Oliver Twist, by Charles Dickens (1812–70), was first published in episodes in a popular magazine in 1838. In the story, Oliver Twist, an orphan, is brought up in a workhouse until the age of nine. He avoids being given to a chimney sweep as an apprentice but instead is made to work for an undertaker where he is bullied and teased about his mother. He escapes and is befriended by the pickpocket, the Artful Dodger, who takes him to his leader, Fagin.

Source A Charles Dickens' description of a poor district of London in his novel, *Oliver Twist*

> A dirtier or more wretched place he [Oliver Twist] had never seen. The street was very narrow and muddy, and the air was impregnated with filthy odours. There were a good many small shops; but the only stock in trade appeared to be heaps of children, who, even at that time of night, were crawling in and out at the doors, or screaming from the inside…Covered ways and yards…disclosed little knots of houses, where drunken men and women were positively wallowing in filth; and from several of the door-ways, great ill-looking fellows were cautiously emerging…

Source B A description of Fagin

> a very old shrivelled Jew, whose villainous-looking and repulsive face was obscured by a quantity of matted red hair. He was dressed in a greasy flannel gown, with his throat bare…

How we imagine these times has been influenced by Dickens whose stories are still popular today and have been made into films, television serials and musical comedies. But what do they tell us about real people and what it was like to live then?

Source C
Second-hand shoe dealers in Dudley Street, Seven Dials, London in 1872 by Gustave Doré

Investigations

1 What does this novel tell you about
  a) the kinds of stories the public enjoyed?
  b) attitudes then towards
  • children in Oliver's situation,
  • Jews (Source **B**)?

2 Suggest other kinds of evidence historians could use to check Dickens' description of London in 1838.

3 How does Doré's picture (Source **C**) show that conditions in poor areas of London had changed little 34 years after Dickens wrote *Oliver Twist* (Source **A**)?

4 Of what use are novels like *Oliver Twist* to historians?

Key words

Apprentice Someone working for a skilled person in order to learn a trade.

Paintings

St James's Church in Bristol belonged to the Church of England. It made money by allowing a fair to be held on its land every year and charging the public tolls to get in. The fair had a bad reputation for crime and **immorality**. Many local people and Nonconformist churches wanted to ban the fair. Samuel Colman, a local artist and Nonconformist, painted this picture as a comment on the evils of this fair. St James's Fair was stopped eventually in 1838.

Source A *St James's Fair*, (1824) by Samuel Colman

Investigations

1 Compare the left half of the picture with the right. What differences can you spot between:
  a) the buildings?
  b) the trees?
  c) the people?

2 Look at the left half of the picture. Find and suggest why the artist has painted the following:
  a) a man looking at a racing calendar
  b) the shop assistant holding the hourglass in front of the woman looking at the mirror
  c) the woman in the red cloak receiving a letter from a hidden man.

3 The artist uses traditional symbols or emblems which have special meanings. Can you find and suggest why he uses the following:
  a) a broom. 'Jumping the broom' is an old expression meaning to elope, or marry without parent's permission.
  b) broken eggshell at the feet of the old woman who is showing the necklace to the girl. This was a symbol of lost innocence.
  c) a boy spitting out orange peel. The skin of an orange looks attractive but tastes bitter; it is a symbol of being tricked, tempted or distracted by appearances.

4 Find the angry-looking farmer (wearing a smock, bowler hat and carrying a stick). Who do you think he is looking for and why?

5 Of what use are paintings as evidence to historians?

Key words

Immorality Behaviour thought to be sinful, such as gambling or prostitution.
Nonconformist A Protestant who is not a member of the Church of England.

Maps

By comparing old maps it is possible to see how a place has changed over time. Old maps like these can be found in museums and reference libraries. Sources **A** and **B** show the same area in the centre of the port of Bristol in 1581 and 1828. Notice the change in the way maps were drawn.

To help you match key points on the maps the numbers 1 and 2 have been added.

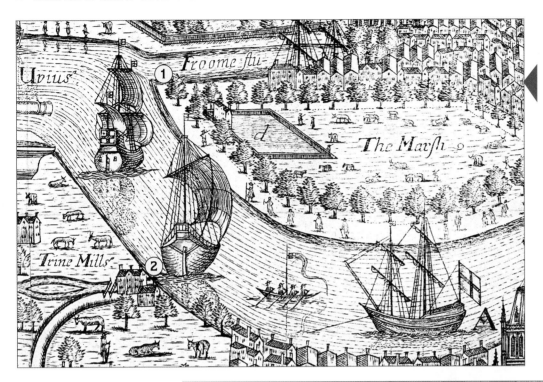

Source A A section from Millerd's view of Bristol, 1673

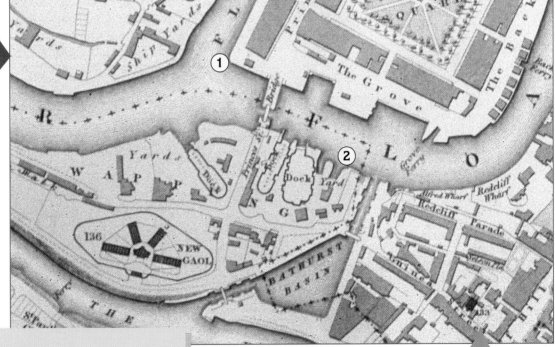

Source B A section of Ashmead's map of Bristol, 1828

Key words

Flu River.
Marſh Marsh.
Dry dock A dock emptied of water and used to build, clean or repair ships.
Basin A waiting area for ships passing through locks.

Investigations

Compare Sources **A** and **B**. Find and describe five changes.

Local Authority Record Offices

Local Authority Record Offices look after many different kinds of local records including private papers left by individuals.

The Horwood Book

At the Bristol Record Office are the papers of Dr Richard Smith (Source **A**) who worked at the Bristol Royal **Infirmary** in 1821. These papers include a book bound in leather made from the skin of an executed criminal whose body was handed over to Richard Smith for dissection and public lectures on anatomy. The evidence in the book shows that Smith played a key part in the arrest and trial of the executed man whose name was John Horwood. However, it also shows that Horwood may not have been guilty of the crime for which he was hanged.

Source A   Dr Richard Smith

Source B   A sketch of John Horwood drawn at his trial

John Horwood, who was 18, was accused of murdering his ex-girlfriend, Eliza Balsam. Witnesses said that he had threatened her with violence several times and that once he had thrown a bottle of acid over her clothes. On 26 January 1821, between 8 p.m. and 9 p.m., Horwood is said to have thrown a stone which hit Eliza on the side of the head.

Source C   A sketch map drawn for the trial, showing where Horwood and two companions were seen, standing on a hill, some 40 yards (36 metres) away when the stone hit Eliza

Despite bleeding badly, Eliza, helped by two friends, managed to run to her brother Richard's house about 8 yards (7 metres) away. The wound was about the size of a man's thumbnail. Her brother cut the hair off the wound with a pair of scissors, shaved it, and afterwards applied a plaster of salt butter. The next day Eliza was seen fetching water from a well and carrying the bucket (weighing about 22 kilograms) on her head. She did this several times. However, later she was vomiting and in great discomfort. Five days later she walked with her sister from Hanham to the Bristol Royal Infirmary (about 5 miles) where she was treated by Dr Richard Smith. He decided to drill a hole in her head to lift the bone off her wound which had gone septic. He then applied to the Bristol magistrates to have Horwood arrested.

After a violent struggle, Horwood was brought to Eliza's bedside to be formally identified by her as the person who caused her wound. She died shortly afterwards.

Dr Richard Smith gave evidence that the stone thrown at Eliza caused her death. Horwood's execution took place on top of the gatehouse of the new gaol in front of a very large crowd. The next day Smith took away Horwood's body for dissection and public lectures on anatomy, which lasted four days. Afterwards he kept Horwood's skull to make measurements for a phrenological chart (Source **D**) to put inside the book bound with his skin.

Phrenology was a so-called science which was supposed to be able to tell a person's character and intelligence from the size and shape of the head, and the weight of the brain. According to Horwood's chart he was aggressive and liked himself a lot but 'the bump of murder' was not developed.

Source D Horwood's phrenological chart

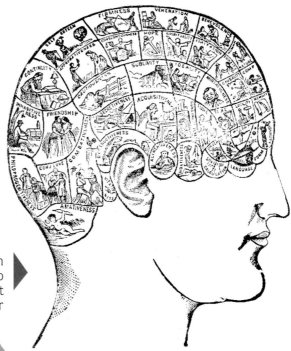

Source E An illustration from a popular handbook on phrenology published in 1869. The head was divided up into different areas or 'organs', each of which was thought to affect character or behaviour

Investigations

1 Find the time and date when Eliza was hit by the stone and look at Source **C**. Why would it be difficult to prove today that Horwood threw the stone and intended to murder her?

2 What evidence is there that it may not have been just the stone which caused Eliza's death?

3 If you had been a lawyer defending Horwood at his trial, who would you have questioned and what questions would you have asked?

4 Why do you think Richard Smith kept evidence of Horwood's trial and execution and his phrenological chart?

Key words **Infirmary** Hospital.

Census

The first accurate **census** of the population of Britain took place in 1801. Since then there has been a census every ten years.

Source **A** is a summary from the 1851 Census of the population growth from 1801 for the village of Henbury (then a part of Gloucestershire). The people who collected information for the census (Census Enumerators) went from house to house and wrote the information into special books (Source **B**). Though the figures from these enumerators' books became a part of the published census the books themselves remained unpublished.

Source A Population of the village of Henbury, adapted from the 1851 Census

	1801	1811	1821	1831	1841	1851
Males	208	207	191	172	189	193
Females	229	240	240	218	253	241
Total population	437	447	431	390	442	434

However, it is still possible to look at them (usually on microfilm) in reference libraries or Record Offices. The most detailed and precise books date from 1851.

Name and Surname of each Person	Relation to the Head of Family	Condition	Age (Male)	Age (Female)	Rank, Profession or Occupation	Where Born
House No. 3.						
William Fenner	Head	Mar	36		Bootmaker master employing 2 & P.S	Gloucestershire - Clifton
Caroline "	Wife	Mar		38		Somerset, Bath
Alfred "	Son		6		Scholar	Gloucestershire ~ Henbury
Elizabeth "	daughter			4	" at home	" "
John "	Son		2			" "
James "	Son		1			" "
James Hulbert	Nephew	U	23		Boot and shoe maker	" "
Eli Frott	Apprentice	U	18		" " "	N. Petherton
House No. 4						
Hannah Lee	Head	Widow		74	Sextoness	Northumberland, Morpeth
Catherine Bunting	Sister			72	Assistant	" "
Fanny Rossland	Granddaughter	U		21	Scholar at home	Gloucestershire, Clifton
House No. 14						
Edward Samson	Head	Mar	40		Magistrate; Landed proprietor	Gloucestershire, Henbury
Belinda "	Wife	Mar		38		Bucks, Denham
Charlotte Powell	Servant	U		40	Cook and Housekeeper	Monmouthshire
Grace Richards	"	U		26	Ladies Maid	Somersetshire, Abbotsleigh
Lisan Pamber	"	U		39	House Maid	Herefordshire
Julia Berry	"	U		19	House Maid	Gloucestershire, Acton Turville
Ellen Williams	"	U		15	Kitchen Maid	" Almondsbury
Henry Wilde	"	U	25		Butler	" Henbury
Charles Sams	"	U	17		Page	" Henbury

Source B House numbers 3, 4, and 14 adapted from the 1851 Census Enumerator's book for Henbury

Remember...

- Interesting investigations into the past can start with novels, paintings, old maps, documents and objects left by individuals and censuses.
- Useful places to find primary evidence apart from museums and art galleries, are public reference libraries and Public Record Offices.

Key words

Census An assessment or count of a population.
Scholar A school child or student.
Sextoness A female sexton; a church caretaker.

Investigations

1 Look at Source **A**.
a) What do you notice about the number of females compared with males?
b) A cholera epidemic hit Henbury. In which year do you think this happened and why?
c) Between 1801 to 1851 the population of Britain grew by 73 per cent. Why do you think the population of Henbury did not grow as fast?

2 Look at Source **B**.
a) What different kinds of information does the enumerator's book give about the people living in Henbury in 1851?
b) What evidence is there that the people living in house 14 were richer than the people living in houses 3 and 4?

7 ◆ Protest and reform
Religion

Why did religion cause so much argument?

Many people argued that the Church of England should no longer be the official Church of the United Kingdom. There was much to complain about:

- The following could not be MPs or achieve high positions in public life: Nonconformists (until 1828); Roman Catholics (until 1829) and Jews (until 1858).
- People objected to compulsory church rates – taxes which went to the Church of England.
- Up to 1880 Nonconformists in many areas had to bury their dead in Church of England graveyards using the Church of England funeral service.
- To many it seemed the Church of England favoured the rich and middle classes and tolerated evils like the slave trade, poor working conditions and poverty.

John Wesley (1703–91) tried to put the Church back in touch with ordinary people. He travelled the country and preached in a simple way so that people could understand the Christian message. Opposition to his methods by the Church of England forced him to start his own Methodist Church in 1784. William Wilberforce (1759–1833) believed loss of support for the Church of England was a cause of unrest in 1797 at a dangerous time when an invasion was expected from France. He was one of the leaders of the **Evangelicals** who aimed to revive support for the Church of England by setting an example of Christian behaviour by campaigning to end the slave trade and improve the lives of the poor.

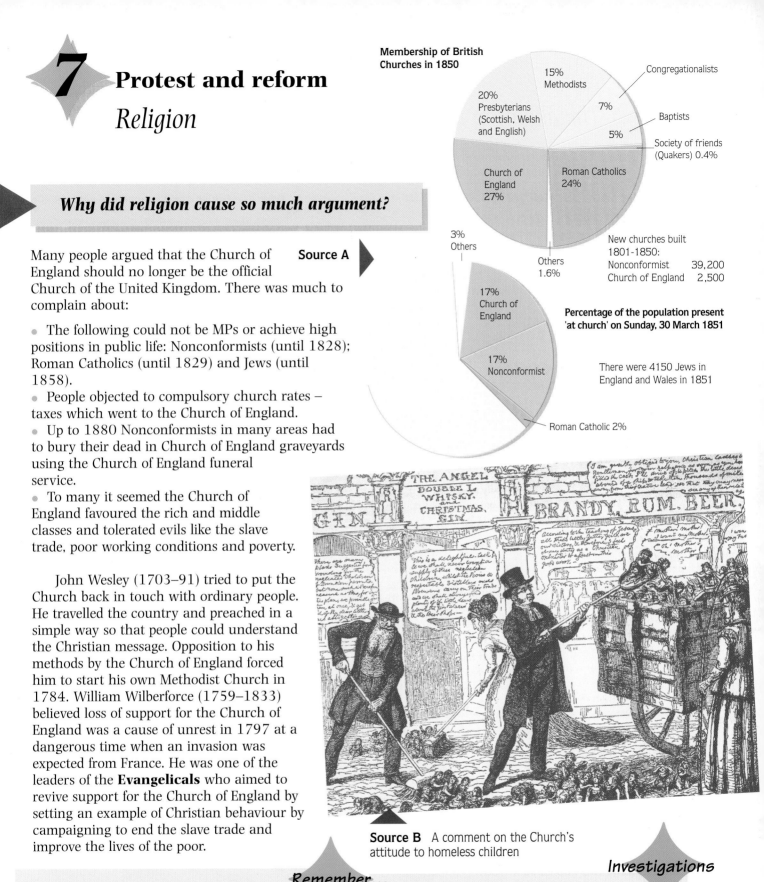

Source A ▶

Membership of British Churches in 1850

- 15% Methodists
- 20% Presbyterians (Scottish, Welsh and English)
- Congregationalists 7%
- Baptists 5%
- Society of friends (Quakers) 0.4%
- Church of England 27%
- Roman Catholics 24%
- 3% Others

New churches built 1801–1850:
Nonconformist 39,200
Church of England 2,500

- Others 1.6%
- 17% Church of England
- 17% Nonconformist
- Roman Catholic 2%

Percentage of the population present 'at church' on Sunday, 30 March 1851

There were 4150 Jews in England and Wales in 1851

Source B A comment on the Church's attitude to homeless children

Remember...

- **Religion continued to play a very important part in the politics of the United Kingdom.**

Investigations

1 How does Source **A** help explain why many people objected to the Church of England being the official Church?

2 What would an evangelical Christian have thought about the comment Source **B** is making on the attitude of the Christian minister?

Key words

Evangelical Someone who tries to inspire faith by sharing knowledge of the Gospels and setting a good example of Christian behaviour.

The abolition of slavery

> The British slave trade may be said to have been doomed when Sharp, Clarkson, Wilberforce and their little band of **propagandists** opened their countrymen's eyes to the brutalities it involved.
>
> From *The British Anti-Slavery Movement*, 1933

Why was the campaign to end the British slave trade a success?

Reginald Coupland (Source **A**) believed that individuals like William Wilberforce were responsible for ending the slave trade. Other historians have disagreed. For example, in 1944 the West Indian historian, Eric Williams, argued that slave labour produced more sugar than was needed and so there was less money to be made from slavery. Then in 1975 Roger Anstey (Source **C**) suggested that the campaigners used the war with France as a reason to persuade Parliament to stop British traders selling slaves to the French islands in the West Indies.

Source B How the slave trade worked

NORTH AMERICA

Slaves sold

Slave ships returned to Britain loaded with cotton, tobacco, sugar and rum

CUBA

JAMAICA

Slaves sold

The slave trade made a number of families in Bristol and Liverpool very rich

Specially built slave ships carried wrought iron, cotton cloths, glass, wines and gunpowder to trade for slaves

African slave traders caught and brought the slaves to the European traders who waited for them at the coast. Ships of 150 tons could carry up to 100 slaves packed on shelves

'Seasoning period' Up to another $\frac{1}{3}$ slaves died before being auctioned like cattle to work on farms called plantations which grew sugar cane, cotton and tobacco

'The middle passage' The voyage across the Atlantic took up to eight weeks during which it was not unusual for one in three slaves to die

AFRICA

> The key to the abolition is the way in which the abolitionists [thought up]…the tactic…to present the abolition of up to two thirds of the British slave trade as [in] the national interest in time of war.
>
> From *The Atlantic Slave Trade and British Abolition*, 1975

Source C By historian, R. Anstey

Investigations

Remember…

- The slave trade was abolished in 1807 before slavery ended in Britain and its colonies in 1833.

1 Which information in Source **A** matches Source **B**?

2 **a)** How do the three historians' interpretations of the abolition of slavery differ?
b) Why do you think these historians have discovered different interpretations of the abolition of slavery?
c) Which of these historians' interpretations do you find the most convincing and why?

Key words

Abolition The ending of the slave trade.
Propaganda Information spread to persuade people what to think about a cause or a government.

Peterloo

Source A An eyewitness describing the arrival of people at St Peter's Field

Peterloo

On a hot afternoon on 16 August 1819 a crowd of 60 000 gathered for a public meeting at St Peter's Field near the centre of Manchester (Source **A**). Many were Nonconformists. Among them was a cotton spinner, John Lees. He had learned to read in a Methodist Sunday school and had fought in Wellington's army at the battle of Waterloo. They came to listen to a well-known speaker, Henry Hunt, share his ideas on **reforms** such as giving all men the right to vote and ending bribery and corruption at elections. The meeting was advertised in the *Manchester Observer*, a newspaper which supported the reformers.

The magistrates, who included two Church of England priests, ordered a cavalry troop of part-time volunteers to arrest Hunt and disperse the crowd. The soldiers killed 11 people and wounded over 500. The Prince Regent and Home Secretary thanked the magistrates for doing a good job.

One of the victims was John Lees. Had he died on the battlefield at Waterloo his name would have been forgotten. The inquest on his death received a lot of publicity which helps explain why what happened at St Peter's Field came to be called the Peterloo massacre.

The consequences

The government reacted by passing six tough laws in December 1819 to
- ban meetings of more than 50 people.
- ban marching and weapon practice.
- punish insults to the Church and government.
- increase a tax on newspapers.
- allow magistrates to search homes for weapons and documents without permission.
- make it faster to take people to court and punish them.

Key words

Libel Any writing which damages a person's reputation.
Magistrate Justice of the Peace.
Reform To change something for the better.

The 'marching order', of which so much was said afterwards, was what we often see now in the processions of Sunday school children…Our company laughed at the fears of the **magistrates**, and the remark was, that if the men intended mischief they would not have brought their wives, their sisters, or their children with them.

From *Historical Sketches and Personal Recollections* by A. Prentice, 1851

Source B A cartoon published in December 1819 showing the rights of a Free Born Englishman

The Cato Street Conspiracy, 1820

Source **C** shows the attic of a house in Cato Street, London, in 1820. A gang is about to be arrested for plotting revenge for Peterloo. They had been set up by a police spy called George Edwards who not only recruited members of the gang for their leader, Arthur Thistlewood, but suggested a plan to murder the entire cabinet of government ministers as they sat at dinner together in a house in Grosvenor Square.

Edwards introduced Thistlewood to William Davidson who bought the weapons for the gang. Davidson was born in Kingston, Jamaica in 1786 where his father was the island's white **Attorney-General** and his mother a slave. Educated in England, he was press-ganged into Nelson's navy. Afterwards he became a skilled cabinet maker. For a time he also taught in a Methodist Sunday school.

During the arrest Thistlewood stabbed and killed a Bow Street Runner (the first kind of uniformed London policeman). Davidson fired a shot and lunged with a cutlass at the commander of the raiding party.

The judge sentenced Thistlewood, Davidson and three other plotters to be hanged, beheaded and cut into four quarters. Only the last part of the sentence was not carried out. Half an hour after they were hanged their heads were cut off and held up to show the crowd. It was the last public decapitation in Britain.

Source C
The Cato Street
Conspirators, 1820

Key words

Attorney-General Chief lawyer.
Conspirators Members involved in a plot.

Remember...

• **The government reacted to the Peterloo massacre by reducing people's rights.**

Investigations

1 Study Source **A** on page 79.
  a) Why do you think the crowds arrived in 'marching order'?
  b) Does Source **A** prove the magistrates over-reacted? Explain your answer.

2 What rights does Source **B** on page 79 suggest people did not have at the end of 1819?

3 What did John Lees (page 79) and William Davidson (page 80) have in common?

4 Which of the people in Source **C** (labelled 1, 2 and 3) are
  a) the Bow Street Runner
  b) Thistlewood and
  c) Davidson.

5 Why is Source **C** of value to historians as evidence about the Cato Street conspirators and their arrest?

6 Explain who you think was really responsible for the Cato Street Conspiracy.

Ned Ludd and Captain Swing

Who were 'Ned Ludd' and 'Captain Swing'?

Before the invention of factory machines spinning and weaving were skilled jobs which people could do in their own homes. The new machines in the textile factories in Lancashire, Nottingham and Yorkshire could be operated by fewer, lower paid and unskilled workers.

In 1811–12 letters signed 'Ned Ludd' appeared (Source **A**). It was a false name to protect desperate workers who carried out their threats (Source **B**).

Source B A newspaper report

O n Friday afternoon, about four o'clock, a large body of rioters suddenly attacked the weaving factory belonging to Messrs Wroe and Duncroft, at West Houghton [Lancashire]…They instantly set it on fire, and the whole of the building with its valuable machinery…were utterly destroyed…The reason for this horrid act is, as at Middleton, 'weaving by steam'…

From the _Annual Register_, April 1812

Source C Swing rioters ▶

The Government sent 12 000 troops to the troubled areas to prevent the Luddite violence turning into a revolution.

Enclosures (see page 38) had taken away labourers' rights to farm common and waste land and to glean fields of any corn left by the harvesters. This made it even more difficult to survive hard times. In 1830 and 1831 bad harvests pushed up food prices, forced landowners to raise rents and caused farmers to cut wages. Landowners, farmers and parish priests received threats by farm workers using the name 'Captain Swing' backed up by attacks on their property.

Source A Letter sent to an employer in the textile industry

Sir
Information has just been given that you are a holder of those detestable **shearing-frames** and I was asked by my men to write to you and give fair warning to pull them down. If they are not taken down by the end of the week I shall send at least 300 men to destroy them.

Signed, Ned Ludd

Remember…

- Luddites and Swing rioters made threats, smashed machines, and damaged property in protest against loss of jobs and poverty.

Investigations

1 What did 'Ned Ludd' and 'Captain Swing' have in common?

2 What clues do Sources **A**, **B** and **C** give about the motives for their threats and attacks?

Key words

Shearing-frame Machine used for quickly clipping wool off sheepskin, which replaced hand-held shears.
Tithe Church tax.

Trade unions

The Tolpuddle Martyrs

Farmers in the village of Tolpuddle in Dorset broke a promise to keep wages the same as other labourers' wages in Dorset – about 10 shillings (50p) a week. Even worse, in 1832 they cut wages to 8 shillings a week which was not enough to live on. In 1833 the Tolpuddle farm labourers formed a trade union called the Tolpuddle Friendly Society as an alternative to violent protest.

Trade unions collect funds to help out their members in hard times and during strikes. The Combination Acts (1799–1800) banning trade unions had been ignored. Parliament made trade unions legal again in 1824 in the hope that this would stop workers plotting in secret and improve relations with their employers.

However, to become a member of the Tolpuddle Friendly Society each labourer had to swear an oath on the Bible. A magistrate, much hated for his part in crushing the Swing rioters (see page 81), got to hear of this (Source **A**). His name was James Frampton.

On 24 February 1834 six members of the Tolpuddle Friendly Society were arrested. Three of them including their leader, George Loveless, were also Methodist preachers. All but one, James Hammett, were witnessed by an informer taking part in the swearing of oaths. A judge sentenced them to seven years of hard labour in Australia (Source **B**).

Source A Notice put up in Tolpuddle by James Frampton on 22 February 1834

> **A**ny person who shall administer, or be present at...or taking an unlawful oath...WILL BECOME GUILTY OF **FELONY** AND BE LIABLE TO BE TRANSPORTED FOR SEVEN YEARS (Mutiny Act 1797).

Source B What judge John Williams said at Dorchester Assizes, 19 March 1834

> **I** am not sentencing you for any crime you have committed, or that could be proved that you were about to commit, but as an example to the working class of this country.

This judgement led to protests everywhere but it was not until 1836 that the six men were given a royal pardon. Five returned in 1838 (Source **C**). The sixth, James Hammett, did not return until 1839.

Source C The Returned Convicts in *Cleave's Penny Gazette*, 12 May 1838. The Tolpuddle **Martyrs** were welcomed as heroes on their return to Britain.

New Model Trade Unions

Low paid workers like the farm labourers of Tolpuddle found it difficult to raise enough money to run a trade union. The most successful trade unions had members who were skilled workers like the **Amalgamated** Society of Engineers (ASE), formed in 1851. These became models for other unions to copy. Their membership card (Source **D**) gives clues to explain why.

Key

1 Goddess of Fame
2 & **3** Brothers proving that 'Unity is strength'
4 Samuel Crompton, inventor of the spinning mule
5 James Watt, improver of the steam engine
6 Richard Arkwright, inventor of the water frame
7, 8, 9, 10, 11 and **12** Five branches of the iron trade

Source D Membership certificate of the Amalgamated Society of Engineers, 1851

Notice the mixture of trades brought together in the ASE. Look at their motto: 'Be United and Industrious'. 'Industrious' means hard work. Hard work won respect. Members of unions like the ASE wanted to be respectable and use strikes only as a last resort. Only workers who could afford to pay 1 shilling a week (5p) could join. Members of the ASE earned on average 10 shillings (50p) more than policemen, miners and dockers and twice as much as farm labourers. A large amount of the money was saved in case of a strike but some of it paid for a full-time general secretary and for sick pay and pensions. At this time pensions and sick pay were not paid for out of taxes. This alone made trade unions like the ASE worth joining.

Remember...

- In 1834 six farm labourers from Tolpuddle suffered the punishment of transportation to make an example of them for forming a trade union.

- From 1851 trade unions organised by skilled workers became models for success.

Key words

Amalgamated Joined together.
Felony A serious crime.
Martyr Someone who suffers for doing what they think is right.

Investigations

1 **a)** What is the difference between the reason the Tolpuddle men were arrested (Source **A**) and the reason they were punished (Source **B**)?
   b) Why do you think the Tolpuddle men were treated as heroes on their return (Source **C**) and are remembered as martyrs today?

2 From which different trades and industries did the Amalgamated Society of Engineers draw its members (Source **D**)?

3 Why did unions like the Amalgamated Society of Engineers stand more chance of survival than the Tolpuddle Friendly Society?

Philanthropy, co-operation and self-help

Who helped the poor?

Philanthropists

Philanthropists are individuals who devote their lives to doing good. Two examples are Lord Shaftesbury (1801–85) and Mary Carpenter (1807–77).

Lord Shaftesbury (Source **A**) was a Church of England evangelical. First as Tory MP, Anthony Ashley Cooper, then as Lord Shaftesbury from 1851 (when he inherited his title), he used his influence in Parliament to help bring about Factory Acts in 1833, 1840, 1844 and 1850, the Mines Act of 1842 and the Chimney Sweeps Act of 1875. These banned children under the age of nine from working in factories, made the employment of children as chimney sweeps illegal, limited women to 12 hours of paid work a day, and stopped women and boys under 13 working underground in mines. He also helped set up the Young Man's Christian Association (YMCA) and ragged schools (Source **B**) to give poor boys an education and a chance to learn a trade.

Mary Carpenter was a Unitarian – a Nonconformist who tolerated other religions so long as they believed in God as one person or being. She believed that education for young people was a better solution to crime than prison (Source **C**).

In Bristol she set up a ragged school (1846), a reformatory school for boys and girls (1852) and the first reformatory school for girls only (1854). Then in 1866 she made the first of three visits to India to promote the education of women (Source **D**).

Source A Extract from Lord Shaftesbury's diary

E very one must take that in which his circumstances will give him the best means of doing good…and I am bound to try what God has put into me for the benefit of old England.

Source B A ragged school in London

T he only school provided in Great Britain by the State for her children, is – THE GAOL…It would seem that the walls of this school-house are rather unnecessarily thick and massive to confine the limbs of a tender child.

From *Reformatory schools for the children of the perishing and dangerous classes*, 1851

Source C
Mary Carpenter's views on the education of young people

Source D Extract from Mary Carpenter's diary, 8 January 1866

A grand and new life appears opening to me…of going to our distant India, and there working…for the elevation of women, and perhaps for the planting of a pure Christianity.

How did working people help themselves?

At this time the most important thing was to be thought respectable. To be respectable meant not having to live off charity or enter a workhouse or turn to crime. It meant being independent through self-help. The secret of self-help was hard work, **thrift**, and improvement through education. Pictures like Source **E** and books on self-help became best sellers.

In Rochdale poor weavers co-operated together to form 'the Rochdale Society of Equitable Pioneers' in 1844. Members paid 2*d*. (0.8p) a week. With these funds they bought goods to sell. They rented and then bought houses and land to make and grow the goods. The idea was also to create jobs. Profits were used to keep prices low. Some were put back into the business, and the rest was spent on social services like reading rooms (Source **F**).

Source E 'Industry and Idleness' by Henry Heath, 1851

Source F From *The History of Co-operation* by G.J. Holyoake, written in 1906

I n the large shop [in Rochdale]...three men are chopping and serving meat in the butcher's department with from twelve to fifteen customers waiting...the newsroom has twenty or more men and youths reading the newspapers.

Source **G** shows how quickly the Rochdale example was copied.

Source G
Membership of Co-operative Societies

1851	150,000
1875	473,000
1900	1,701,000

To avoid competition the 'Co-ops' joined together to form Co-operative Wholesale Societies in England in 1863 and in Scotland in 1868.

Remember...

- **Many poor people avoided the workhouse or charity through self-help, thrift and co-operation.**

Key words   **Thrift** Careful saving and managing of money.

Investigations

1 a) Find clues in Sources **A**, **B**, **C** and **D** which show what inspired Lord Shaftesbury and Mary Carpenter to do good?

2 a) What does Source **B** tell us about
- the condition of the children who attended ragged schools?
- the equipment used?

- methods of teaching and learning?
b) What likely problems are not shown in this picture?

3 Suggest why pictures like Source **E** became best sellers?

4 How do you explain the increase in members of Co-operative Societies shown in Source **G**?

Chartism

The wealthy landowners who controlled Parliament (see page 8) feared that the respectable middle classes would become the leaders of a revolution supported by the working classes. So, from 1832 they made it possible for middle-class men to vote in elections and join them in Parliament. Men qualified to vote if they owned or rented property worth just more than most working-class people could afford. Discontented leaders and supporters of the working class responded with a campaign called Chartism. It started in 1839 with a petition to Parliament listing six demands which became known as the People's Charter. They demanded:

1 The vote for all men over 21.
2 Voting in secret (secret ballot) to protect the voter.
3 No need to own property to become an MP.
4 Payment of MPs.
5 All voting districts to have the same number of voters.
6 A general election every year.

Moderate leaders of the Chartists wanted to persuade Parliament by peaceful methods and hoped that MPs would take notice of this petition when they saw how many people had signed it. Other leaders, like Feargus O'Connor, were more aggressive.

Source B George Cruickshank's cartoon shows how he imagined the scene in the House of Commons if the Charter was accepted

Source A The views of Feargus O'Connor, a lawyer and Chartist leader

> H e would always have working people bear in mind, that it is better to die freemen than to live like slaves. Every conquest which was honourable had been achieved by physical force.
>
> **From the *Northern Star*, September 1838**

Parliament rejected the Charter in 1839, 1842 and in 1848. The third rejection coincided with revolutions in Europe. Fearing that a plan for a mass Chartist rally in London would lead to trouble the Duke of Wellington organised troops to defend the city.

THE CHARTER - A Common's Scene.

Investigations

1 How do clues in Sources **A** and **B** and some of the six demands help to explain why Parliament rejected the People's Charter?

2 Find out how many of the Chartists' demands have now been accepted.

Remember...

- **The Chartists wanted the vote for working-class men but were split about how to achieve their aims.**

The Opium War 1839–42

Why was protest against Britain's part in the Opium War ignored?

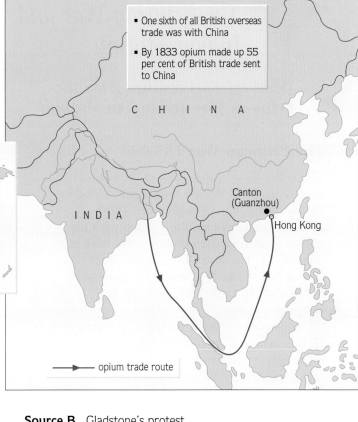

- One sixth of all British overseas trade was with China
- By 1833 opium made up 55 per cent of British trade sent to China

C H I N A

I N D I A

Canton (Guanzhou)

Hong Kong

→ opium trade route

Source A
The opium trade route from India to China

Tea, which came from China, had become the most popular drink with the British working class. The tea was paid for with **opium** grown in India (Source **A**). Drug addiction in China from smoking opium became so serious a problem that the Emperor made growing, importing or smoking opium illegal. The punishment was death by public strangulation.

In 1838 British merchants rescued a Chinese opium smuggler who was about to be executed. The Chinese reacted by making 200 merchants prisoners in their own trading station in Canton (Guanzhou) until all their stocks of opium were handed over to be destroyed. Nevertheless, the merchants continued to smuggle opium. The next year the Chinese surrounded two English ships with 29 war **junks** after the British had refused to hand over a sailor for the murder of a Chinese man. The British opened fire and sank four of the Chinese ships. The Opium War had begun.

British politicians argued that by interfering with private property and free trade China was guilty of a worse crime than trading in opium. An exception was William Gladstone MP who protested against Britain's part in the war (Source **B**).

Source B Gladstone's protest

> We the **enlightened** and civilised Christians, are pursuing objects at variance with justice and religion.
>
> From *Hansard*, 8 April 1840

The British easily defeated the Chinese who up to this time had allowed them to trade only in the Port of Canton. The Chinese were forced to sign a peace treaty in 1842 in which they agreed:
- to open up five ports (including Canton) to British trade.
- to pay for the confiscated opium and the cost of the war.
- to give Britain the island of Hong Kong.

Key words

Enlightened Informed and unprejudiced.
Junk A flat-bottomed sailing ship with a square prow.

Opium An addictive drug produced from the white poppy which was smoked for pleasure and also used as a medicine to relieve stress or pain.

Investigations

Remember...

- **The result of the Opium War was that Britain increased its trade with China and took over the island of Hong Kong.**

1 Why did Gladstone protest against the war with China (Source **B**)?

2 Why do you think Gladstone's protest was ignored?

The Crimean War and Indian Mutiny

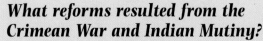

What reforms resulted from the Crimean War and Indian Mutiny?

The Crimean War 1854–6

When Russia declared war on the Ottoman Empire in 1853 Britain and France came to its assistance. On 14 September 1854 British troops invaded the Crimea with the aim of capturing the Russian naval base at Sebastopol. The war ended in defeat for Russia but showed up serious weaknesses in the British Army and its medical services.

Newspaper reports on the war reached Britain within days of being sent by telegraph or steam ship by *The Times* war correspondent, William Howard Russell

The Ottoman Empire controlled the straits (waterway) which gave the Russian navy its only access to sea which was not frozen for part of the year.

Source A The Crimean War

Source B Report in *The Times*, 14 October

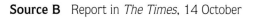

I t is with surprise and anger that the public will learn that no sufficient preparations have been made for the wounded.

A team of nurses led by Florence Nightingale soon arrived to improve conditions at the military hospital at Scutari followed by a new prefabricated hospital building specially designed by Brunel.

Meanwhile, the Jamaican nurse, Mary Seacole, won admiration for her bravery and skill in looking after wounded soldiers on the battlefield.

Russell's report on a disastrous cavalry charge, led by Lord Cardigan (Source **C**), at the Battle of Balaclava was one of several reports which led to improvements and changes in military training after the war.

Source C Russell's report in *The Times*, 14 November 1854

O ur loss…in killed, wounded, and missing at two o'clock today, was as follows:

Went into action	Returned from action	Loss
607	198	409

Source D The Charge of the Light Brigade – 'A Trump Card(igan)', published in *Punch*, 1854

The Indian Mutiny 1857

British power in India depended on the loyalty of Indian soldiers, known as sepoys, who outnumbered British soldiers in the army by five to one. In 1857 sepoys and civilians in the North Eastern part of India turned on the British when 85 sepoys in Meerut were punished for refusing to load the new Enfield rifle with a cartridge greased in animal fat made from beef and pork. This greatly offended Hindus for whom the cow is a sacred animal and upset Muslims who reject meat from pigs as unclean. The violence was sudden and horrific (Source **F**).

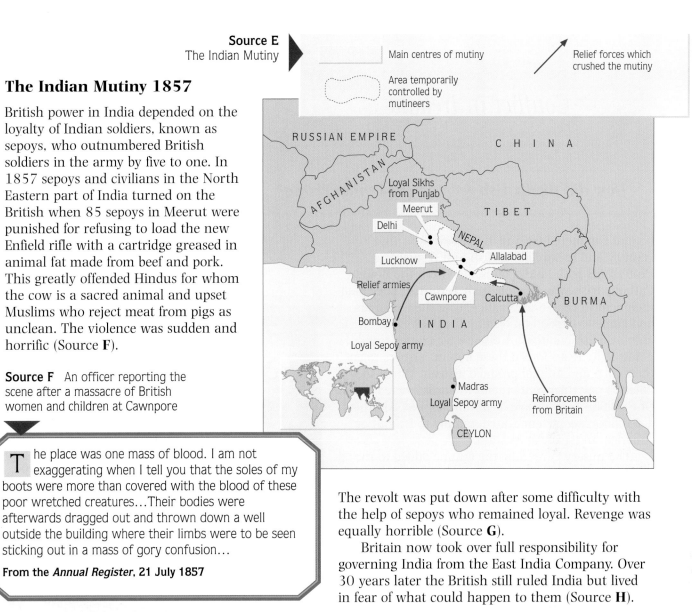

Source E
The Indian Mutiny

Main centres of mutiny

Area temporarily controlled by mutineers

Relief forces which crushed the mutiny

Source F An officer reporting the scene after a massacre of British women and children at Cawnpore

> The place was one mass of blood. I am not exaggerating when I tell you that the soles of my boots were more than covered with the blood of these poor wretched creatures…Their bodies were afterwards dragged out and thrown down a well outside the building where their limbs were to be seen sticking out in a mass of gory confusion…
>
> **From the *Annual Register*, 21 July 1857**

The revolt was put down after some difficulty with the help of sepoys who remained loyal. Revenge was equally horrible (Source **G**).

Britain now took over full responsibility for governing India from the East India Company. Over 30 years later the British still ruled India but lived in fear of what could happen to them (Source **H**).

JUSTICE.

Source G 'Justice', published in *Punch*, 12 September 1857

Source H The wife of a civil servant working for the British government in India described how it felt to live in India

> I honestly confess that the overwhelming crowds of people frighten me…What were we in the land…but a handful of Europeans at the best, and what was there to prevent these [people] from falling upon and obliterating us, as if we had never existed?
>
> **From *Letters from India* by Lady Wilson, 1889**

Remember…

- **The Crimean War and Indian Mutiny exposed weaknesses which led to reforms in the British Army and the replacement of the East India Company by the British government as ruler of India.**

Investigations

1 What impact did the following make during the Crimean War:
   a) the telegraph and steam ships;
   b) newspaper reports;
   c) women?

2 How do you explain the attitudes of the British towards Indians shown in Sources **G** and **H**?

3 What lessons did the Crimean War and the Indian Mutiny teach Britain?

Conflict in Ireland

How did the British react to the Fenian rising?

Source A The Fenian Guy Fawkes

THE FENIAN GUY FAWKES.

Britain conquered Ireland in the seventeenth century and rewarded Scottish and English Protestants with lands confiscated from the Roman Catholic Irish who became their **tenants**. They paid their rent in corn and produce from their animals and came to depend on feeding themselves and their animals with potatoes. A disease which destroyed potatoes in 1846 forced these tenant farmers to eat their corn and animal produce instead. When they failed to pay their rents their landlords evicted them. One million Irish people died from famine. Another 1.5 million people emigrated, mainly to Britain or America, to escape starvation.

The misery caused by the famine added to the bitterness and hatred the Irish Catholic majority felt towards Protestants in Ireland and Britain. They wanted to end British rule which had been strengthened by an Act of Union in 1800. The threat of another Catholic rebellion in 1829 was enough to force the British government to allow Roman Catholic MPs in to the British Parliament. However, they were outnumbered by MPs who supported the Protestant Irish who wanted Ireland to remain under British rule. For this reason a revolutionary organisation, called the Irish Republican Brotherhood – the Fenians – was formed in 1858 to fight for Ireland's independence. Irish Catholic sympathisers who had emigrated to America and Britain helped raise money for the IRB.

Terrorist murders and bombs which killed policemen and innocent people in England horrified and angered the British public but forced them to take notice. Source **A** shows one reaction to IRB terrorism in 1867.

British politicians like William Gladstone began to listen sympathetically to the Irish Catholics' point of view.

Remember...

- **The Irish Republican Brotherhood was formed to fight for independence for Ireland as an alternative to peaceful political methods.**

Key words

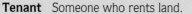

Tenant Someone who rents land.

Investigations

Look at Source **A**.

1 Match the following labels to an outline of Source **A**:
   - IRB terrorist
   - sub-human, unintelligent face
   - a widow
   - orphans

2 How might Catholic Irish people have reacted to this cartoon?

3 What did the Fenians and Guy Fawkes have in common?

Political parties

Why did people vote Conservative or Liberal?

From 1832 the increase in the number of people who could vote in elections (Source **A**) and new rules for elections (Source **B**) made it necessary for politicians to have efficient political party organisations. These aimed to attract new supporters and make sure they registered their right to vote. The Tories and Whigs became the modern Conservative and Liberal parties (Source **C**). The Labour party did not exist until 1900.

Source A Men over 21 who gained the right to vote

Reform Act	Social class	England and Wales	Scotland	Ireland
1832	Middle class	1 in 5	1 in 8	1 in 20
1867	Working class who lived in towns	1 in 3	1 in 3	1 in 6
1884	Farm labourers	2 in 3	3 in 5	1 in 2

Source B Rules which made a difference at elections

1832 Register of electors

The names of those qualified to vote had to be kept on a register.

1854 and 1883

Laws passed to prevent bribery and intimidation of voters.

1872 Secret ballot

Voters no longer had to tell anyone who they voted for.

✦ Conservative
1 Supported Church of England.
2 Supported the monarchy.
3 Supported old ruling class of country landowners.
4 Supported Union between England, Scotland, Wales and Ireland.
5 Wanted to improve the health of the people.
6 Tried to keep a balance of power between foreign countries and avoid alliances.
7 In favour of having an Empire.

✦ Liberal
1 Sympathetic to Nonconformists.
2 Sometimes critical of the expense of the monarchy and its influence in religion and foreign relations.
3 Aimed to reduce taxes.
4 Sympathetic to greater independence for Scotland, Wales and Ireland.
5 Sympathised with foreign countries whose monarchs had limited powers and whose governments were liberal in their views.
6 Supported **free trade**.
7 Saw Empire as an unwelcome responsibility.

Source C The differences between the Conservative and Liberal parties

Remember...

- **Modern political parties developed from 1832.**

Key words

Free trade Trade which is not restricted or protected from competition.

Investigations

1 Who had not gained the right to vote in elections to Parliament by 1900?

2 How do Sources **A** and **B** help to explain the growth of organised modern political parties?

3 Why might working-class people have found it difficult to choose between the Conservative and Liberal parties?

Depth Study: Gladstone and Disraeli

How did Gladstone and Disraeli compare?

Two of Britain's leading politicians between 1832 and 1894 were William Gladstone and Benjamin Disraeli. They were rivals and hated each other.

Source A A biographer describing Gladstone's feelings about Disraeli

G ladstone always denied that he actually loathed Disraeli, but those who knew him best were agreed that at the time his sentiment towards his rival became that of black hatred.

From *Gladstone: a biography* by P. Magnus, 1954

P osterity will do justice to that unprincipled maniac, Gladstone – extraordinary mixture of envy,...hypocrisy and superstition; and with one commanding characteristic – whether praying, speechifying, or scribbling –never a gentleman!

Source B Disraeli describing his feelings about Gladstone in a letter to Lord Derby, October 1876

William Gladstone (1809–98) was the son of a Liverpool millionaire and slave owner whose family originally came from Scotland. Gladstone spoke with a northern accent. He was educated at Eton and Oxford University and was bought a seat in Parliament in 1832. He started his political career as a Tory. He was a strong believer in the Church of England and wrote books on religion. He fell out with the Conservatives because of his support for free trade. From 1847 he was Tory MP for Oxford University who rejected him in July 1865 because of his sympathy with Nonconformists and support for giving the working class the vote at elections (Source **C**). He became Liberal MP for South Lancashire instead. Within three years he was prime minister.

Source C
'Pegasus Unharnessed', published in *Punch*, 29 July 1865. Gladstone is the horse, Pegasus, released from the cart by the angry university professor

PEGASUS UNHARNESSED.

Gladstone's first government as prime minister from 1868–74 is remembered for several important reforms (Source **D**) which did not please everyone. Though he promised to get rid of income tax he lost the general election in 1874 to the Conservatives led by Disraeli and for a while gave up being leader of the Liberal party.

Benjamin Disraeli's father was also a wealthy man. Though Jewish, he made his son become a Christian because he thought this would help his career. Benjamin Disraeli (1804–81) made his name as a novelist and became an MP in 1837.

Source E In a speech in the House of Commons on 15 March 1838, Disraeli said that he did not believe other countries would:

S uffer England to be the workshop of the world.

For this reason, he strongly opposed free trade and favoured protection of trade and expansion of the British Empire. He became leader of the Conservative party and was responsible for working men in towns gaining the vote in 1867.

Source F Disraeli speaking in June 1872 about the Reform Act of 1867

T he discontent upon the subject of representation…was terminated by the Act of Parliamentary Reform of 1867–8. That Act was founded on a confidence that the great body of the people of this country were 'Conservative' that they believe, on the whole, that the greatness and the empire of England are to be attributed to the ancient institutions of the land…

Disraeli's government (1874–80) also passed reforms but is remembered too for his interest in foreign affairs (Source **G**).

Key words

Posterity Those coming after, in the future.
Representation The right to vote, to be represented in Parliament.

Source D The highlights of Gladstone's government 1868–74

✦ **1869 Ireland** The Protestant Church of Ireland ceased to be the established (official) Church of Ireland.

✦ **1870 Education Act** Made schools available for all young children.

✦ **1871 Universities** Nonconformists, Catholics and Jews allowed to become students at Oxford and Cambridge Universities.

✦ **Civil Service** Promotion open to competitive examinations.

✦ **Army** Abolished the buying of officer ranks.

✦ **Trade unions** Laws protected union funds from dishonest officials but banned demonstrations to prevent people from going to work during a strike.

✦ **1872 Elections** Introduced the secret ballot (see page 91).

✦ **Licensing Act** Anyone wishing to sell beer or spirits had to have a licence and could only sell them at certain hours.

✦ **1875 Housing** Local councils got permission to improve the standard of housing.

✦ **Public health** Local authorities had to improve the supply of fresh water and the disposal of rubbish and sewage.

✦ **Chimney sweeps** Young boys could not be employed as chimney sweeps.

✦ **Trade unions** Unions were allowed to peacefully persuade other workers to support strikes.

✦ **Suez Canal** Britain bought the shares in the canal owned by the Khedive (governor) of Egypt.

✦ **1876 India** Queen Victoria became 'Empress of India'.

✦ **1877 Africa** Britain took over the Transvaal from the Boers (white South Africans) and went to war with the Zulus.

✦ **1878 Russia** Disraeli helped save Turkey from defeat by Russia by persuading Turkey to give up control of some parts of its Ottoman Empire.
✦ Britain went to war with Afghanistan to stop Russia gaining a base there from which they could invade India.

Source G The highlights of Disraeli's government 1874–80

The Suez Canal, which was built by the French to link the Mediterranean and Red Sea, opened in 1869. It became very important as a trading route for steamships as it greatly shortened the journey to India. In 1875 Disraeli snapped up the chance to buy the Governor of Egypt's shares in the canal to prevent the French, who owned the other shares, gaining complete control.

Source I 'New crowns for old', published in *Punch*, 1876. Disraeli persuaded Queen Victoria to accept the title 'Empress of India'. She gave him a title in return by making him Lord Beaconsfield

Source H The Suez Canal provided a faster route for steamships to reach India

Steamship route via Suez Canal

Old route before Suez Canal

Disraeli's defence of Turkey outraged Gladstone, who fiercely criticised the Turks for their brutality in Bulgaria in a famous pamphlet which became a best seller. Standing up to the Russians, however, made Disraeli's actions popular, as the music hall song in Source **J** shows.

> We don't want to fight but by jingo if we do,
> We've got the ships, we've got the men,
> We've got the money too.
> We've fought the bear before, and while we're Britons true
> The Russians shall not have Constantinople.

Source J
Music hall song written by G.W. Hunt in 1877

The Suez Canal and Egypt were part of the Ottoman Empire. In 1876 its Turkish rulers reacted to rebellions in Bulgaria, Serbia and Montenegro by brutal massacres. This provoked Russia to act as the protector of the rebels by invading Turkey. Disraeli acted with the leaders of Austria and Germany to prevent Russia completely defeating Turkey.

From this song, the word *Jingoism*, came to describe enthusiasm for the empire and showing off Britain's strength in the world. Feelings like this sickened Gladstone and led to angry quarrels with Disraeli about what was best for Britain (Source **K**).

A BAD EXAMPLE.

DR. PUNCH. "WHAT'S ALL THIS? YOU, THE TWO HEAD BOYS OF THE SCHOOL, THROWING MUD! *YOU OUGHT TO BE ASHAMED OF YOURSELVES!*"

Disraeli died in 1881 but Gladstone went on to become prime minister on three more occasions (1880–5, 1886 and 1892–4). In 1881 Gladstone's attitude to empire was put to the test when rebellion began against all foreigners in Egypt. When Egyptians attacked British property in Alexandria in 1882 Gladstone decided Britain had to take over Egypt to keep control of the Suez Canal (Source **L**).

Meanwhile, Gladstone became obsessed with the idea that he could bring peace to Ireland. He tried to protect farmers from landlords who evicted them or raised rents unfairly (Source **M**). He then turned to the idea of Home Rule which would allow the people of Ireland to govern themselves while Ireland still remained a part of the United Kingdom. This, however, split his own party in 1886 between supporters of Home Rule and those who feared that Home Rule would weaken the Union between Britain and Ireland. From this time onwards the Liberals and Conservatives found it difficult to form governments without the support of MPs who either supported Home Rule or who were Unionists.

Source L
Gladstone invading Egypt

Source M
Gladstone fighting the Irish Devil Fish, published in *Punch*, 18 June 1881

Remember...

- Gladstone led the Liberal party. He believed in free trade, did not think empires were a good thing and tried to give Ireland Home Rule.

- Disraeli led the Conservative party. He opposed free trade and favoured expanding Britain's Empire.

Investigations

Use the evidence in this depth study to organise an election campaign supporting either Gladstone or Disraeli:
a) Decide who you support and find others to form a small group.
b) Use the evidence to make posters and write speeches both supporting your choice and criticising your opponent.
c) At the end of the campaign vote by secret ballot.

8 Empire!

From Workshop to Empire

> ### Why did the British Empire expand?

The Great Exhibition in London in 1851 (see page 40) showed that Britain was the leading industrial and trading nation in the world. However, at the Paris Exhibition in 1867 it became clear that Britain's lead over other nations was slipping. By 1881, Britain was no longer the workshop of the world (Source **A**).

Competition and the loss of markets abroad led to unemployment and hard times at home in Britain (Source **B**).

Source A An economist described the changes affecting British trade

> Thirty years ago…the world was obliged to buy from [England] because it could not buy elsewhere…; now, France and America and Belgium have got machinery, our machinery and our workmen and our capital, and are driving our own goods out of our own markets, and every year are more completely closing their markets to our goods…
>
> **From 'Isolated Free Trade' in *Nineteenth Century* by E. Sullivan, 1881**

Source B 'Unfair Trade Winds' published in *Punch*, 1884

Source C Lord Salisbury, the new Conservative leader, said that Britain's survival as a leading nation now depended on expanding the empire

> Your empire, if we mean it to live, must grow, must steadily grow. If it ceases to grow it will begin to decay.

Source D Cecil Rhodes argued in 1895 that expanding the empire could save Britain from a civil war

> In order to save the 40,000,000 inhabitants of the United Kingdom from a bloody civil war, we colonial statesmen must acquire new lands to settle the surplus population, to provide them with new markets for the goods produced by them in the factories and mines.

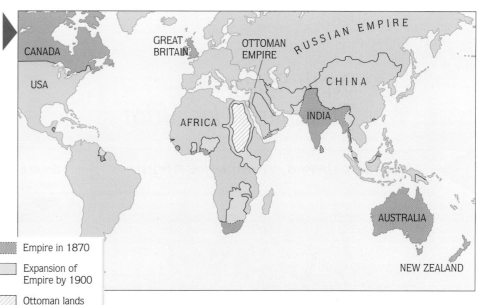

By 1900 the British Empire had dramatically expanded to cover more than one fifth of the world's land surface (Source **E**).

Nevertheless, the number of **emigrants** to the Empire was less than half the number who emigrated to the USA (Source **F**). The export trade to the Empire did not increase greatly (Source **G**) and 80 per cent of imports from the Empire still came from the oldest parts of the Empire like India, Canada, South Africa, Australia and New Zealand.

Empire in 1870

Expansion of Empire by 1900

Ottoman lands under British control

Of the 400 million peoples of the British Empire only about one-eighth were white-skinned. A famous poem summed up the attitude of many white people who helped build the Empire (Source **H**).

Source F Number of people emigrating from the United Kingdom and where they settled

	Total	USA	Canada	Australia/ New Zealand	South Africa	Total Empire	All other countries
1861–70	157	113	13	27	1	41	3
1871–80	168	109	18	30	5	53	6
1881–90	256	172	30	37	8	75	9
1891–1900	174	114	19	13	17	49	11

(Figures are averages per year to the nearest thousand.)
B.R. Mitchell and P. Deane, *Abstract of British Historial Statistics*, CUP, 1962

Source H Written in 1899 by Rudyard Kipling

> Take up the White Man's burden
> Send forth the best ye breed –
> Go bind your sons to **exile**
> To serve your captives' need

But were British white men fit enough to carry this heavy burden of responsibility (Source **I**)?

Source G Where British exports went (as a percentage of total)

Source I
A letter to *The Times* by Lord Rosebery, 1900

> An Empire such as ours requires as its first condition an **Imperial** Race – a race vigorous and industrious and intrepid...The survival of the fittest is an absolute truth in the conditions of the modern world.

	Europe	USA	British Empire	South America	China and Japan
1880–4	33.7	12.2	34.5	6.9	3.1
1910–13	33.6	6.2	35.8	9.6	5.0

Remember...

- **From about 1870 to 1900 Britain's position as 'workshop of the world' began to decline but at the same time the British Empire was transformed into the largest in the world.**

Key words

Emigrant Someone who moves to live in another country.
Imperial Anything to do with empire.
Exile Having to live in a foreign country.

Investigations

1 In which part of the world did the British Empire expand most between 1870 and 1900?

2 How do Sources **A** and **B** help explain the decline of Britain as the leading industrial and trading nation?

3 How does Source **B** help explain Cecil Rhodes' fears of a civil war in Britain (Source **D**)?

4 To what extent do the emigration and trade statistics (Sources **F** and **G**) prove that Lord Salisbury and Cecil Rhodes (Sources **C** and **D**) were right?

5 What different views about the people building the Empire are suggested by Kipling and Rosebery in Sources **H** and **I**?

Depth Study:
The scramble for Africa

Why was there a scramble for Africa?

Source A The dangers and attractions of Africa as seen by Europeans in the 1870s

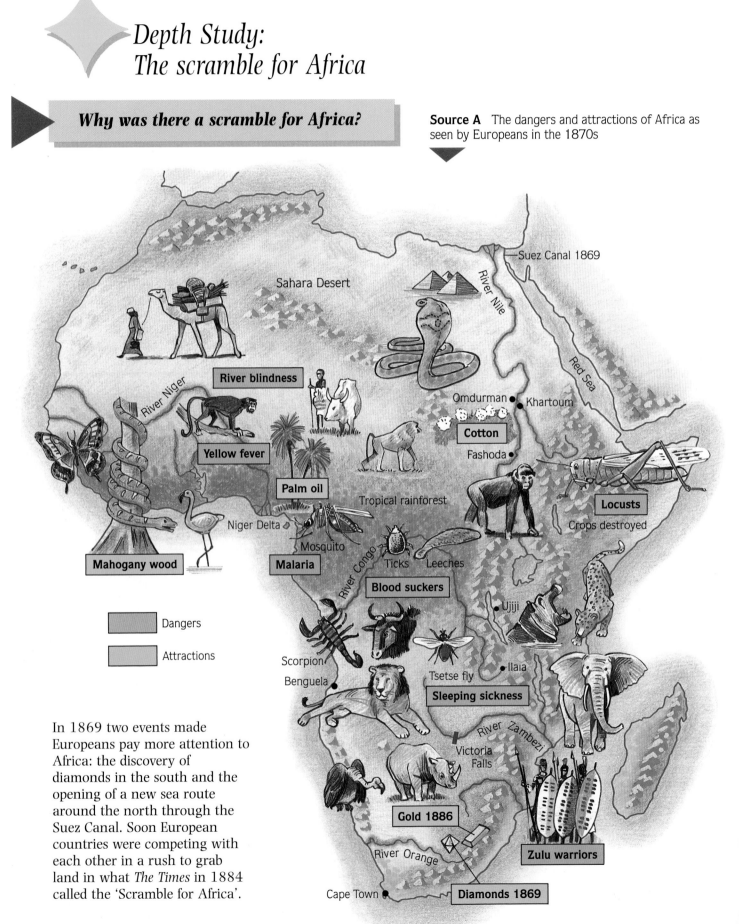

Sahara Desert

Suez Canal 1869

River Nile

Red Sea

River Niger

River blindness

Yellow fever

Palm oil

Omdurman · Khartoum

Cotton

Fashoda ·

Tropical rainforest

Locusts

Crops destroyed

Niger Delta

Mosquito

Ticks   Leeches

River Congo

Malaria

Blood suckers

Ujiji

Mahogany wood

Dangers

Attractions

Scorpion

Benguela ·

Tsetse fly

· Ilaia

Sleeping sickness

River Zambezi

Victoria
Falls

Gold 1886

River Orange

Zulu warriors

Cape Town ·

Diamonds 1869

In 1869 two events made Europeans pay more attention to Africa: the discovery of diamonds in the south and the opening of a new sea route around the north through the Suez Canal. Soon European countries were competing with each other in a rush to grab land in what *The Times* in 1884 called the 'Scramble for Africa'.

Explorers and missionaries

The first Europeans to travel deep into the interior of Africa were explorers and Christian missionaries. Quinine, a drug to overcome the disease malaria, and steamships made this possible. Explorers were interested in finding where the major rivers like the Niger, Zaire (Congo) and Zambezi led, and whether they were linked to the River Nile.

Dr David Livingstone was a Scottish Christian missionary and the first European to cross Africa (Source **B**). Livingstone wanted to open up Africa to put an end to a new slave trade organized by the Swahili and Arabs in East Africa. Books about his work and adventures excited and won the admiration of readers in Britain and America.

When contact with him was lost a New York newspaper sent Henry Morton Stanley to look for him. He found Livingstone working at Ujiji in 1871.

In 1873 another search party looking for Livingstone arrived too late. He had died at Ilala in May. The leader of the search party, Lieutenant Verney Cameron met some of Livingstone's devoted African followers carrying Livingstone's body back to England to be buried. Unable to persuade them to bury him in Africa he continued what proved to be a remarkable journey. It ended in November 1875 on the west coast of Africa near Benguela in Angola. News of what he had discovered on this journey caused great excitement (Source **C**).

Source B Cover of a book about the famous missionary and explorer, Dr Livingstone

Source C From Cameron's notes to the Royal Geographical Society, published in *The Times*, 11 January 1876

The interior is mostly a magnificent and healthy country of unspeakable richness. I have a small specimen of good coal; other minerals such as gold, copper, iron and silver are abundant…

Investigations

1 Find and sort into two lists **ten** dangers and **four** attractions of Africa as seen by Europeans in the 1870s (Source **A**).

2 Describe one clue in Source **B** which shows what attracted Dr Livingstone to Africa.

3 Why did the news of Cameron's discoveries (Source **C**) cause great excitement?

Traders and politicians

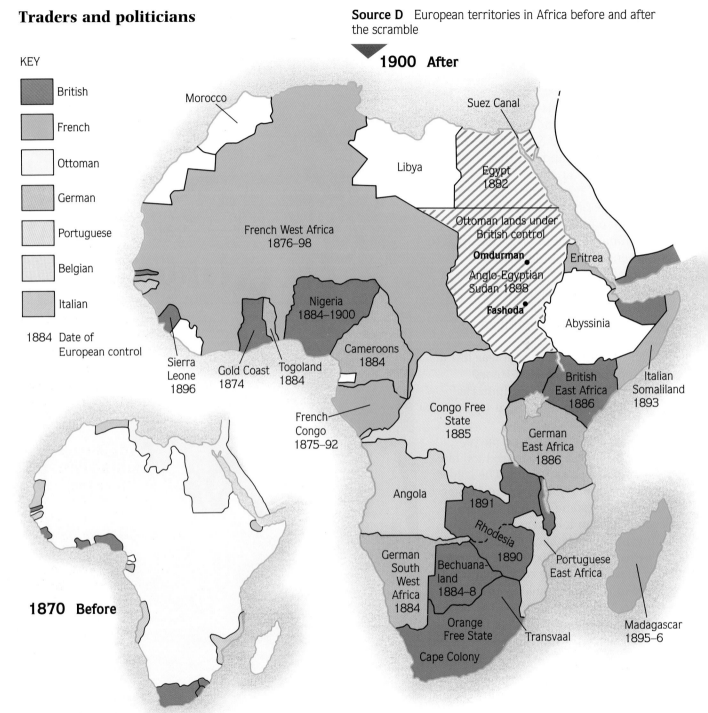

KEY

■	British
■	French
□	Ottoman
▨	German
▨	Portuguese
▨	Belgian
▨	Italian

1884 Date of European control

1900 After

Morocco
Suez Canal
Libya
Egypt 1882
French West Africa 1876–98
Ottoman lands under British control
Omdurman
Eritrea
Anglo-Egyptian Sudan 1898
Fashoda
Abyssinia
Nigeria 1884–1900
Sierra Leone 1896
Gold Coast 1874
Togoland 1884
Cameroons 1884
British East Africa 1886
Italian Somaliland 1893
French Congo 1875–92
Congo Free State 1885
German East Africa 1886
Angola
1891
Rhodesia 1890
Portuguese East Africa
German South West Africa 1884
Bechuana-land 1884–8
Orange Free State
Transvaal
Madagascar 1895–6
Cape Colony

1870 Before

West Africa

The Industrial Revolution and a change in social habits created a big demand for palm oil to lubricate machines and to make soap for washing. The best source of palm oil was the Niger Delta. The palm oil trade became a valuable substitute for the slave trade.

Steamboats made it possible to travel up the River Niger and to set up local trading and collecting centres for palm oil in the interior. Opposition from African traders who feared being put out of business led to the use of force. Then in 1877 a soldier, explorer and trader, George Taubman Goldie, arrived. His ambition was to add the region of the Niger to the British Empire before it was taken over by the French. Within two years Goldie had joined British trading companies in the Niger Delta into one big company. The British government then stepped in to take control of what became Nigeria in 1900.

Central and Southern Africa

Cecil Rhodes (1853–1902) made his fortune out of diamond and gold mines in South Africa. In 1887 he set up the British South Africa Company to develop the region north of the Transvaal which became known as Rhodesia (now Zimbabwe and Zambia). From 1890 to 1896 he served as prime minister of Cape Colony. His ambition was to gain control of Africa from the Cape to Cairo (Source **E**).

Source E The Rhodes Colossus. The cartoon is comparing the size of Cecil Rhodes' ambition in Africa to the gigantic statue at the entrance to the harbour of the Aegean island of Rhodes

In December 1896 Rhodes organised a raid into the Transvaal led by Dr Jameson who was the administrator of Rhodesia. The aim was to stir up a rebellion in the Transvaal against the Boers by foreigners who worked in the Rand gold mines. This would create an excuse to force the Boers to join a Federation of South Africa under British rule. The Boers, who were descended from

Dutch settlers in the Cape, had moved to get away from the British in 1835 and had set up independent homelands north of the Orange and Vaal rivers. To Britain's embarrassment the Boers captured Jameson and his men. On 3 January 1896 the ruler of Germany, Kaiser Wilhelm, sent a telegram from Berlin to congratulate the Transvaal prime minister, Paul Kruger, on beating the British invaders. Rhodes was forced to resign as prime minister of Cape Colony.

Egypt and the Sudan

Rebellion by Egyptians against all foreigners led Britain to occupy Eygpt in 1882 to protect the Suez Canal which was a vital military route to India. Another uprising against Egyptian rule, led by a Muslim leader called the Mahdi, involved Britain in a struggle to regain control of the Upper Nile in the Sudan which supplied essential water to the farmers and cotton growers of Egypt. The struggle is remembered for the death of the British General Gordon in an heroic but unnecessary defence of Khartoum in 1885 and for a famous victory at the battle of Omdurman in September 1898 by General Kitchener which restored control of the Upper Nile to Egypt.

Kitchener's army then marched south for a showdown with a small French force led by Captain Marchand at Fashoda. Marchand was acting on orders to claim parts of the Upper Nile and territories lost by Egypt for France. He had reached Fashoda in July. Aware that this could lead to a major war Kitchener and Marchand telegraphed their governments in London and Paris for advice and drank whisky and champagne together while they waited. In the end it was France who backed down.

By 1900 the scramble for Africa was nearly over.

Investigations

1 **a)** What did each of the following have to do with the scramble for Africa?
   - palm oil, diamonds and gold
   - Cecil Rhodes
   - the Suez Canal
   - competition between European countries
   - quinine and steamships

   b) Which three of the above do you think were the most important causes of the scramble and why?

2 What effect on Britain's relations with France and Germany do you think each of the following had:
   - Kaiser Wilhelm's telegram to Kruger in 1896?
   - the clash with France at Fashoda in 1898?

Remember...

- Between about 1870 and 1900 European countries rushed to take control of parts of Africa. This caused tensions in Britain's relations with France and Germany.

For better or worse?

Inside a working-class home

Sources **A** and **B** show the inside of an iron worker's home in Wales as it might have looked in 1805 and 1895. The house is a part of a row of houses. It has two storeys with a single room on each floor. There is a single storey extension housing a **pantry** and main bedroom. The house did not have taps for running water or an indoor toilet. The houses all shared a single pump for water and a baking oven at the end of the row. Whereas many middle-class homes had gas lighting by 1895, this house had neither gas nor electricity.

Front view

Source A Inside an iron worker's home in 1805

Goffering iron on a stand (for ironing frills)

Flat iron

Rush light holder

Bible

Cross-section

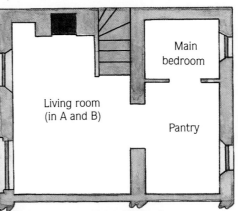

Main bedroom

Living room (in A and B)

Pantry

Ground floor plan

Brass candlestick

Bottle jack (for hanging bottles)

Source B The same scene in 1895

Investigations

1 How many similarities and differences can you spot by comparing Sources **A** and **B**? Copy the headings below and add to the examples in each column:

Changes in an iron worker's home 1805–1895

	Similarities	**Differences**
Example:	Bible	Brass candlesticks

2 Which differences are signs of an improvement in the iron worker's standard of living and why?

3 What developments between 1805 and 1895 made these improvements possible?

Key words

Pantry A store room for food and equipment

103

Awareness of poverty

Why did attitudes change towards poverty?

During the 1880s attitudes towards poverty began to change.

Source A By historian, Arnold Toynbee, speaking in 1883

We – the middle class, I mean, not merely the very rich – we have neglected you; instead of justice we have offered you charity, and instead of sympathy, we have offered you hard and unreal advice…

There were three reasons why poverty began to attract more attention:

- Detailed studies in London by the shipowner, Charles Booth (1889), and in York by the chocolate-maker, Seebohm Rowntree (1901), explained what it meant to be really poor by showing how much money people needed to earn to survive. According to Charles Booth 30 per cent of London's population were below what he described as the poverty line. Seebohm Rowntree came to similar conclusions about York.
- It was impossible in cities like London not to see evidence of poverty (Sources **B** and **C**).
- As Britain's Empire expanded there were worries about the physical fitness of young men. Between 1893 and 1902 over a third of men who volunteered to join the army were rejected as physically unfit. The health of the nation seemed to be getting worse rather than better.

Evidence of poverty

Children often saw more of their older sisters and brothers than their mothers or fathers who worked long hours (Source **C**).

Source B
Children in the East End of London in the 1880s

Most working-class homes had only cold running water from one tap in the yard or kitchen and a toilet in an outhouse in the backyard. Bathtime was a weekly event in a tin tub in front of the fire. The bath water was boiled in pots and kettles and had to be shared with the rest of the family. Washing clothes was a whole day's work. Wash day was often an excuse for keeping girls at home from school to help their mothers.

Cooking was done on a coal stove made of iron with ovens built into the sides and hot plates on top. It was not usual to have a cooked breakfast. Instead people ate bread with jam or dripping (fat saved from cooking). Dinner was put on the stove in the morning – often a stew made from the left-overs of the Sunday roast. In the poorest homes food was taken to a local bakehouse to be cooked.

Health care was not free. People saw doctors only if illness was very serious. Families relied on home cures and local chemists as much as possible. There were no fridges to keep food fresh or free from flies. Germs spread quickly. Rubbish in alleys and cesspits attracted rats. The houses of the poor were difficult to keep free from bedbugs and lice. It was not uncommon for as many as six small children to share a bed in poor homes. Skin infections were very common. There was a high death rate, especially among children, from illnesses such as scarlet fever, measles, whooping cough, tuberculosis, diarrhoea and influenza (flu). Even blood poisoning caused by dirt in small scratches could be fatal.

Source C By George Sims

A t the open door sits a girl of eight...a typical 'little mother' of the London doorstep...She is nursing a heavy baby who is perhaps a year old. She talks to it, soothes it, hushes it to sleep, rocks it, dandles it when it wakes up, and kisses its poor little face again and again. But every other minute her attention is distracted by the conduct of a sister, aged four, and a brother, aged five...Because she is the oldest of all that have come, all that come after her are hers to tend and hers to watch.

From *How the Poor Live*, 1883

Remember...

- **By 1900 there was evidence of an improvement in standards of living inside working-class homes since 1750. However, the upper and middle classes were becoming more aware of poor living conditions and standards of health among the working classes, especially in cities like London and York.**

Investigations

1 Whose attitude towards the poor changed in the 1880s, according to Source **A**?

2 Look at the clothes and feet of the children in Source **B**. What evidence of poverty is there in this photograph?

3 What are the possible dangers of the situation described in Source **C**?

Depth Study: Women

▶ Was this an age of improvement for women?

Women were the property of men. The marriage service confirmed this when a father handed over his daughter to her husband and she promised to obey him. Selling of wives, although rare, was not unknown. Thomas Hardy makes use of this shocking fact in the beginning of his novel, *The Mayor of Casterbridge*, when Michael Henchard puts his wife, Susan, up for auction at a fair (Source **A**).

Source A   The sale of a wife in *The Mayor of Casterbridge*, published in 1886

> **F**ive guineas,' said the auctioneer, 'or she'll be withdrawn. Do anybody give it? The last time. Yes or no?'
> 'Yes,' said a loud voice from the doorway.
> All eyes were turned. Standing in the triangular opening which formed the door of the tent was a sailor.

AN '

MR. Bu

During the 1800s women gradually gained some important legal rights (Source **B**). However, Parliament refused to give them the right to vote in elections or to become MPs.

Source C   A cartoon showing the fight for equal rights in 1870

Source B   Rights for women

✦ **1839** If a man left his wife she was allowed to keep all the children under the age of seven.

✦ **1848** Women could attend London University.

✦ **1857** Women could divorce their husbands for cruelty and desertion but not for adultery, even though their husbands could divorce them for adultery. Women who divorced their husbands gained some legal rights to property.

✦ **1870** Women who earned money were allowed to keep £200 but had to give the rest to their husbands. Girls between 5 and 13 had the same right to go to school as boys.
✦ Women joined the Boards which helped to run schools.

✦ **1876** Women could go to medical schools.

✦ **1882** A wife could own property and do what she liked with it.

✦ **1884** A wife ceased to be the property of her husband and became an independent separate person.

✦ **1886** Husbands had to pay money to support their wives if they left them.

✦ **1891** Women could not be forced to live with their husbands.

✦ **1894** Women gained the vote in parish council elections.

Clever women were looked upon as freaks of nature and troublemakers. The education of boys was given priority over that of girls. In the novel, *The Mill on the Floss* by George Eliot, Mr Tulliver asks his friend Mr Riley for advice on the best school to send his son Tom but has no plans to do the same for his daughter, Maggie, who is much cleverer (Source **D**).

Source D   By George Eliot

> **a** woman's no business wi' being so clever, it'll turn to trouble…'
>
> **From *The Mill on the Floss*, 1860**

The author's real name was Mary Ann Evans who, like other women, felt it necessary to use a man's name for her work to be taken seriously.

Source E   A comment on the first women doctors in Britain, 1865. Elizabeth Garrett Anderson, the first British woman to qualify as a doctor, had to take her medical examinations in Paris because of opposition from the male medical profession in Britain.

Few trade unions welcomed women (Source **F**). Many men saw women as a threat to their jobs and wages. One way to make jobs for men was to pass laws like the Mines Act of 1842 to 'protect' women from dangerous work underground. This greatly upset many of the 2 400 women in Scotland who lost their jobs in the mines. It was not until 1885 that the TUC agreed that where women did the same work as men they should receive equal pay.

In 1888 a strike by women at the Bryant and May match factory in London (Source **G**) was one of the first successful strikes by non-skilled workers.

Source F The Trades Union Congress (TUC) which represented most trade unions, speaking in 1877

> The duty of men and husbands is to bring about a condition of things when their wives should be in their proper sphere of home instead of being dragged into competition…with the great and strong of the world.

Source G Annie Besant and the match girls strike committee, 1888

Key words

Socialist Someone who believes in socialism: a system in which wealth is owned and shared fairly by all who do the work to make it.
Rectory The home of a parish priest.

A journalist, Annie Besant, described conditions at Bryant and May's match factory in London as 'White Slavery' (Source **H**).

Source **H** Annie Besant's description of working conditions, published in the newspaper she produced, *The Link*, 23 June 1888

The time for starting work is 6.30 in summer and 8 in winter; work finishes at 6 p.m. Half an hour is allowed for breakfast and an hour for dinner. This long day of work is performed by young girls who have to stand the whole time.

A typical case is that of a girl of 16...she earns 4 shillings (20p) a week and lives with a sister...who earns 9 shillings a week. Out of the earnings 2 shillings is paid for the rent of one room; the child lives on only bread and butter and tea...

If the feet are dirty, or the ground under the bench is left untidy a fine of 3*d*. is inflicted...and in some departments a fine of 3*d*. is inflicted for talking.

A few days later Bryant and May sacked four girls for giving this information to Annie Besant. The other 1400 workers went on strike. Bryant and May were furious (Source **I**).

Source **I** One of the directors of Bryant and May said about the strikers

I have no doubt they have been influenced by the TWADDLE OF MRS BESANT and other **socialists**.

From *The Star*, 6 July 1888

They threatened to sue Annie Besant for libel. However, other journalists visited Bryant and May's factory and reported that she was telling the truth. The public sent money to help the strikers. Bryant and May gave in and the girls went back to work.

Remember...

- **Women did not have the right to vote in elections or to become MPs.**

Thousands of other women were not protected by a trade union or helped by people like Annie Besant. Among the most unfortunate of these were domestic servants who worked as maids and cooks in the homes of the middle and upper classes (Source **J**).

Source **J** Alice Cairns, a maid working for a parish priest, described her work

There was no gas or anything in the **rectory**. The place was lit with oil lamps; and I had to clean the big range and get the fire going before I could boil a kettle. And then I used to scrub the big kitchen which had a floor like gravestones, and scrub the tables, and then take the cook a cup of tea before seven...They used to have huge dinners at nine o'clock at night, which used to go on till ten or ten thirty, before dinner was over, and me being the in-between maid, had all the washing-up to do...We had one day a month off.

Meanwhile, in ordinary homes work for women continued while men relaxed (Source **K**).

Source **K** By Grace Foakes

My mother did not have much pleasure but I do not remember her ever complaining – except on Sunday afternoons when father would undress and get into bed, leaving her to mend his working clothes while he had a rest.

From *Between High Walls*, 1974

Investigations

1 Look at Sources **A** and **B** on page 106. When did it become illegal to do what Michael Henchard did to his wife?

2 **a)** What link is there between Source **C** (on page 106), which shows the women pushing at the door wearing spectacles, and Source **D** on page 107?
   b) Look at Source **E** on page 107. Does the man look ill? Notice the way he looks at the doctor. What attitude towards women doctors does this cartoon suggest?

3 How do Sources **G** (on page 108), **H** and **I** show how Annie Besant helped in the match girls strike in 1888?

4 Work in small groups. Use the sources in this unit to act out scenes in the lives of women at this time.

10 The end of an era?
The Boer War 1899–1902

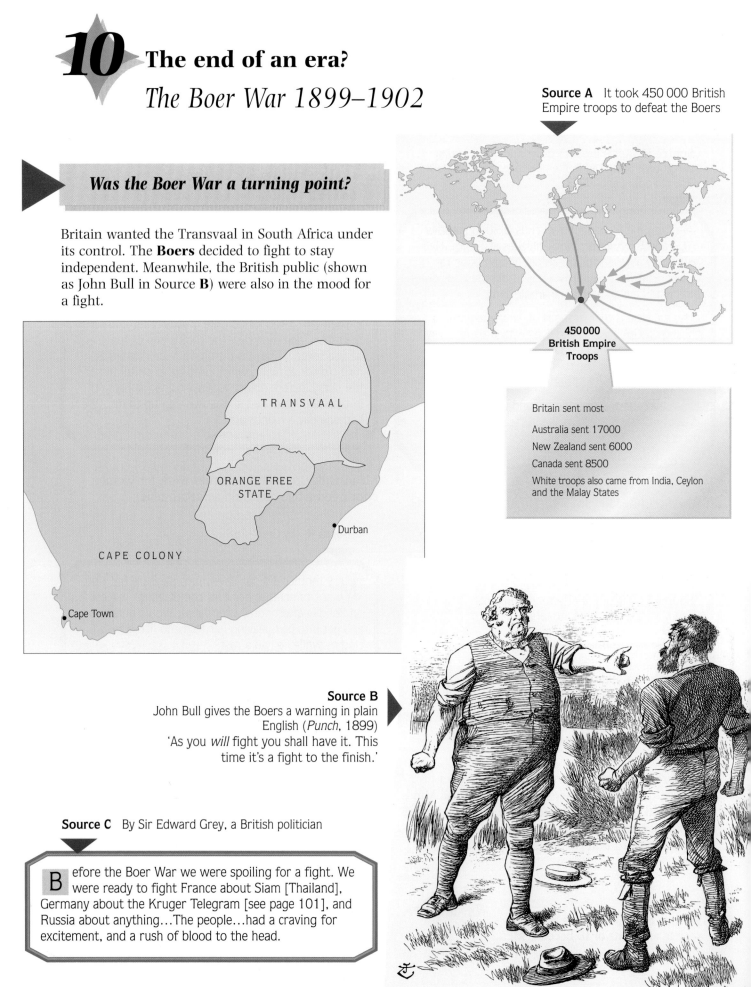

Was the Boer War a turning point?

Britain wanted the Transvaal in South Africa under its control. The **Boers** decided to fight to stay independent. Meanwhile, the British public (shown as John Bull in Source **B**) were also in the mood for a fight.

TRANSVAAL

ORANGE FREE STATE

•Durban

CAPE COLONY

•Cape Town

450 000
**British Empire
Troops**

Britain sent most

Australia sent 17000

New Zealand sent 6000

Canada sent 8500

White troops also came from India, Ceylon and the Malay States

Source B
John Bull gives the Boers a warning in plain English (*Punch*, 1899)
'As you *will* fight you shall have it. This time it's a fight to the finish.'

Source C By Sir Edward Grey, a British politician

Before the Boer War we were spoiling for a fight. We were ready to fight France about Siam [Thailand], Germany about the Kruger Telegram [see page 101], and Russia about anything…The people…had a craving for excitement, and a rush of blood to the head.

It was more difficult to defeat the Boers than expected. The Boer soldiers used their knowledge of the countryside to hide from the British and make surprise hit-and-run attacks. In desperation the British burned the Boers' farms, rounded up their families and put them into concentration camps. In these camps 28 000 Boer women and children died from typhoid, measles (which killed many of the children) and dysentery, caused by poor sanitation and poor diet. The cruelty of the British towards the Boers shocked people all over the world. Many British people lost their enthusiasm for 'empire'.

Source D   By the British politician, David Lloyd George, in June 1901

W hen children are being treated in this way and dying,…it will always be remembered that this is the way British rule started here…the method by which it was brought about.

In the end Britain won what seemed a small victory which cost the British taxpayer £200 million: the Boers accepted defeat with a promise of future self-government. 4000 Boer soldiers lost their lives compared with 7792 British Empire troops who died fighting and a further 1300 who died from illness, mainly diarrhoea. The poor performance of the British Army showed up Britain in front of its main rivals, France and Germany.

Key words

Boers   White South Africans descended from Dutch farmers who settled in South Africa.
Capitalism   A system in which wealth is owned by individuals who make it by employing people to work for them in competition with others.

Investigations

1 a) What impression do Sources **B** and **C** give about Britain's self-confidence in 1898?
   b) Why did David Lloyd George criticise Britain's methods of defeating the Boers (Source **D**)?
   c) Look at Source **E**. What lesson do you think Kipling thought Britain had learned from the Boer War?

2 Look at Source **F**. Why is Capitalism shown as a vampire and Socialism shown as an angel?

3 Which do you think was more of a turning point and why: the Boer War or the death of Queen Victoria?

Source E   *The Times* published a poem in July 1901 by Rudyard Kipling called 'The Lesson'

W e have forty million reasons for failure, but not a single excuse.
So the more we work and the less we talk the better the results we shall get –
We have had an imperial lesson; it may make us an empire yet!

The Labour party

Meanwhile, the Boer War also drew attention to the poor physical state of many British soldiers. These men now returned home to unhealthy living and working conditions. Yet Britain was one of the wealthiest countries in the world. So in 1900 socialists (see page 108) and trade unions got together to form the Labour party to elect MPs to speak for working people.

Source F   Socialism shown as the angel of the labouring man

The old Empress, Queen Victoria, died in January 1901. It was the end of an era in which Britain had been transformed from Workshop to Empire.

Remember…

- **Britain's poor performance in the Boer War shook its confidence as a great power. It turned more attention to political and social problems in Britain.**

Index